BY CHARLES BUKOWSKI

The Days Run Away Like Wild F ⸺ the Hills (1969)

Post Office (1971)

Mockingbird Wish Me Luck (197

South of No North (1973)

Burning in Water, Drowning ⸺ (1974)

Factotum (1975)

Love Is a Dog from Hell: Poems 1974–1977 (1977)

Women (1978)

You Kissed Lilly (1978)

Play the piano drunk Like a percussion Instrument Until the fingers begin to bleed a bit (1979)

Shakespeare Never Did This (1979)

Dangling in the Tournefortia (1981)

Ham on Rye (1982)

Bring Me Your Love (1983)

Hot Water Music (1983)

There's No Business (1984)

War All the Time: Poems 1981–1984 (1984)

You Get So Alone at Times That It Just Makes Sense (1986)

The Movie: "Barfly" (1987)

The Roominghouse Madrigals: Early Selected Poems 1946–1966 (1988)

Hollywood (1989)

Septuagenarian Stew: Stories & Poems (1990)

The Last Night of the Earth Poems (1992)

Screams from the Balcony: Selected Letters 1960–1970 (Volume 1) (1993)

Pulp (1994)

Living on Luck: Selected Letters 1960s–1970s (Volume 2) (1995)

Betting on the Muse: Poems & Stories (1996)

Bone Palace Ballet: New Poems (1997)

The Captain Is Out to Lunch and the Sailors Have Taken Over the Ship (1998)

Reach for the Sun: Selected Letters 1978–1994 (Volume 3) (1999)

What Matters Most Is How Well You Walk Through the Fire: New Poems (1999)

Open All Night: New Poems (2000)

Beerspit Night and Cursing: The Correspondence of Charles Bukowski & Sheri Martinelli (2001)

The Night Torn Mad with Footsteps: New Poems (2001)

Sifting Through the Madness for the Word, the Line, the Way: New Poems (2002)

CHARLES BUKOWSKI

WAR ALL THE TIME

POEMS 1981-1984

ecco

An *Imprint* of HarperCollins*Publishers*

HarperCollins books may be purchased for educational, business, or sales promotional use. For information, please write: Special Markets Department, HarperCollins Publishers Inc., 10 East 53rd Street, New York, NY 10022.

Some of these poems have appeared in the following magazines: *Blow, Electrum, Long Shot, Poetry L.A., Poetry Now, Random Wierdness, Sepia* and *Wormwood Review.* Grateful acknowledgment is made to the editors.

First Ecco edition published in 2003.

Library of Congress Cataloging-in-Publication Data

ISBN 0-87685-638-5
ISBN 0-87685-637-7 (PBK.)

HB 01.24.2023

for Darrell Vienna

Table of Contents

▲▲

▲▲

▲▲▲

war all the time

some of my readers
▲▲▲

I liked it coming out of that expensive
cafe in Germany
that rainy night
some of the ladies had learned that I
was in there
and as I walked out well-fed and
intoxicated
the ladies waved
placards
and screamed at me
but all I recognized was my
name.

I asked a German friend what they were
saying.

"they hate you," he told me,
"they belong to the German Female
Liberation Movement . . . "

I stood and watched them, they were
beautiful and screaming, I
loved them all, I laughed, waved,
blew them kisses.

then my friend, my publisher and my
girlfriend got me into the car; the
engine started, the windshield wipers
began thrashing
and as we drove off in the rain
I looked back
watched them standing in that
terrible weather
waving their placards and their
fists.

it was nice to be recognized
in the country of my birth, that

was what mattered
most . . .

▲▲▲

back at the hotel room
opening bottles of wine
with my friends

I missed them,
those angry wet
passionate ladies
of the night.

talking to my mailbox...
▲▲▲

boy, don't come around here telling me you
can't cut it, that
they're pitching you low and inside, that
they are conspiring against you,
that all you want is a chance but they won't
give you a
chance.

boy, the problem is that you're not doing
what you want to do, or
if you're doing what you want to do, you're
just not doing it
well.

boy, I agree:
there's not much opportunity, and there are
some at the top who are
not doing much better than you
are
but
you're wasting energy haranguing and
bitching.

boy, I'm not *advising*, just suggesting that
instead of sending your poems to me
along with your letters of
complaint
you should enter the
arena—
send your work to the editors and
publishers, it will
buck up your backbone and your
versatility.

boy, I wish to thank you for the
praise for some of my
published works
but that

13

has nothing to do with
anything and won't help a
purple shit, you've just got to
learn to hit that low, hard
inside pitch.

this is a form letter
I send to almost everybody, but
I hope you take it
personally,
man.

the last generation

▲▲

it was much easier to be a genius in the twenties, there were
only 3 or 4 literary magazines and if you got into them
4 or 5 times you could end up in Gertie's parlor
you could possibly meet Picasso for a glass of wine, or
maybe only Miró.

and yes, if you sent your stuff postmarked from Paris
chances of publication became much better.
most writers bottomed their manuscripts with the
word "Paris" and the date.

and with a patron there was time to
write, eat, drink and take drives to Italy and sometimes
Greece.
it was good to be photo'd with others of your kind
it was good to look tidy, enigmatic and thin.
photos taken on the beach were great.

and yes, you could write letters to the 15 or 20
others
bitching about this and that.

you might get a letter from Ezra or from Hem; Ezra liked
to give directions and Hem liked to practice his writing
in his letters when he couldn't do the other.

it was a romantic grand game then, full of the fury of
discovery.

now

now there are so many of us, hundreds of literary magazines,
hundreds of presses, thousands of titles.

who is to survive out of all this mulch?
it's almost improper to ask.

I go back, I read the books about the lives of the boys

and girls of the twenties.
if they were the Lost Generation, what would you call us?
sitting here among the warheads with our electric-touch
typewriters?

the Last Generation?

I'd rather be Lost than Last but as I read these books about
them
I feel a gentleness and a generosity

as I read of the suicide of Harry Crosby in his hotel room
with his whore
that seems as real to me as the faucet dripping now
in my bathroom sink.

I like to read about *them*: Joyce blind and prowling the
bookstores like a tarantula, they said.
Dos Passos with his clipped newscasts using a pink type-
writer ribbon.
D. H. horny and pissed-off, H. D. being smart enough to use
her initials which seemed much more literary than Hilda
Doolittle.

G. B. Shaw, long established, as noble and
dumb as royalty, flesh and brain turning to marble. a
bore.

Huxley promenading his brain with great glee, arguing
with Lawrence that it wasn't in the belly and the balls,
that the glory was in the skull.

and that hick Sinclair Lewis coming to light.

meanwhile
the revolution being over, the Russians were liberated and
dying.
Gorky with nothing to fight for, sitting in a room trying

16

to find phrases praising the government.
many others broken in victory.

now

now there are so many of us
but we should be grateful, for in a hundred years
if the world is not destroyed, think, how much
there will be left of all of this:
nobody really able to fail or to succeed—just
relative merit, diminished further by
our numerical superiority.
we will all be catalogued and filed.
all right . . .

if you still have doubts of those other golden
times
there were other curious creatures: Richard
Aldington, Teddy Dreiser, F. Scott, Hart Crane, Wyndham
        Lewis, the
Black Sun Press.

but to me, the twenties centered mostly on Hemingway
coming out of the war and beginning to type.

it was all so simple, all so deliciously clear

now

there are so many of us.

Ernie, you had no idea how good it had been
four decades later when you blew your brains into
the orange juice

although
I grant you
that was not your best work.

17

windy night
▲▲

they smile and bring the food
they smile and bow
as a light hurricane rattles the
blinds

as the scarlet ibis appears
and dances in the guano
on my plate

I'm not hungry anyhow

Leda, Tyndareus, Clytemnestra,
Castor, Pollux or anybody else
I know wouldn't
eat this stuff.

I ask for a doggy bag.
they smile and scoop the meal
into there.

later in my kitchen I divide
the meal onto their plates
place them upon the floor

as my 3 cats remain motionless
staring up at me
as I ask them, "What's the matter?
What's the matter? Eat it!"

the hurricane scratches
branches against the window
as I switch out the kitchen
light
walk out of there and into
the other room
switch on the tv
just as a cop shoots a
man at the top of a fire escape

18

and he falls and falls
toppling and flattening in the
street:

he will never have to eat
Szechwan shrimp with Chinese
peas
again.

19

here I am
▲▲

drunk at 3 a.m. at the bottom of my 2nd bottle
of wine, I have typed from a dozen to 15 pages of
poesy
an old man
maddened for the flesh of young girls in this
dwindling twilight
liver gone
kidneys going
pancreas pooped
top-floor blood pressure

while the fear of wasted years
laughs between my toes
no woman will live with me
no Florence Nightingale to watch
over me.

if I have a stroke I will lay here for six
days, my three cats hungrily ripping the flesh
from my legs, wrists, head

the radio playing classical music.

I promised myself never to write old man poems
but this one's funny, you see, excusable, be-
cause there's
still more left
here at 3 a.m. and I am going to take this sheet from
the typer
pour another glass and
insert another
make love to the fresh new whiteness

maybe get lucky
again

first for
me

later
for you.

training for Kid Aztec
▲▲

I was a young guy in Los Angeles.
there were little bars
around the Plaza, small Mexican
bars, and there was one large
one, well-frequented, and I
started the night out there
but it was too mellow
full of decent working types
so I got out
found a winding little alley,
dark
and I followed it down
switchblade in pocket until
I found this little bar
at the alley's end
went in
sat on a stool and ordered a
bottle of beer.
there were 4 Mexicans in there
including the bartender
and I sat looking straight
ahead
lifting my beer now and
then.

I was a crazy son of a bitch
ready to go all the way
better not fuck
with me . . .

I finished the bottle
ordered another.

"where the hell are the
women?" I asked.

no answer.

"I shouldn't be in here,"
I said, "I'm training for a
fight at the Olympic, a four-
rounder, I'm fighting Kid
Aztec..."

silence.

I got off my stool, stood
up, sneered, "anybody here want
to spar a little, huh?"

no answer.

I put a coin in the
juke box.
the music came on and
I shadow boxed to
it.

when the piece was
finished I sat down and
ordered another beer.

"I'm a killer," I told
the barkeep, "a born
killer... I'm sorry for
Kid Aztec..."

the barkeep took my
money, rang it into the
register
his back to me.

I said to his
back: "on top of
everything, I'm a writer.

I write short stories,
novels, poems,
essays . . . "

"Señor, you write
poems?" asked a big
Mexican at the end of the
bar.

"shit, yes . . . "

"what do you write these
poems about?"

"love . . . "

"oh, *love*, Señor?"

"love poems to
Death . . . "

I drained my bottle,
ordered another.

"*I* write too,
Señor . . . "

"oh yeah?"

"oh yes, I stick my pencil into
women and I write
inside of them."

the other Mexicans
laughed.
I waited until they were
finished.

24

"you guys are *fools*, you
laugh like *fools*!"

"maybe so, Señor, but even fools
have a right to laugh,
no?"

I peeled the label off
my beer, stuck it face down on
the bar, finished
off the bottle.

"another beer, Señor?" asked
the barkeep.

"naw, that's enough, I got to
get my rest . . ."

I walked toward the
exit.

"good luck with your fight with
Kid Aztec, Señor," somebody
said.

▲▲▲

I walked up the little
alley, stopped to puke in a
dark corner, finished, walked
out on the street
looking for a poem, a better
bar, something,
anything.

I had only bored them with
my dangerousness.

all the nights were the
same and the days were
worse.

I stood under a tree at
the edge of the Plaza
lighting a cigarette and
trying to look like a
killer.

nobody noticed.

maybe they never
would.

I had held the match
too long, it burned my
fingers.
I cursed loudly, stepped
out and began walking
toward the train
station

somebody had told me
that the hookers were
sucking them off right on the
loading ramps . . .

Sparks

▲▲

the factory off Santa Fe Ave. was
best.
we packed heavy lighting fixtures into
long heavy boxes
then flipped the boxes into stacks
six high.
then the loaders would
come by
clear your table and
you'd go for the next six.

ten hour day
four on Saturday
the pay was union
pretty good for unskilled labor
and if you didn't come in
with muscles
you got them soon enough

most of us in
white t-shirts and jeans
cigarettes dangling
sneaking beers
management looking
the other way

not many whites
the whites didn't last:
lousy workers
mostly Mexicans and
blacks
cool and mean

now and then
a blade flashed
or somebody got
punched-out

27

management looking
the other way

the few whites who lasted
were crazy

the work got done
and the young Mexican girls
kept us
cheerful and hoping
their eyes flashing
messages
from the
assembly line.

I was one of the
crazy whites
who lasted
I was a good worker
just for the rhythm of it
just for the hell of it
and after ten hours
of heavy labor
after exchanging insults
living through skirmishes
with those not cool enough to
abide
we left
still fresh

we climbed into our old
automobiles to
go to our places
to drink half the night
to fight with our women

to return the next morning
to punch in

28

knowing we were
suckers
making the rich
richer

we swaggered
in our white t-shirts and
jeans
gliding past
the young Mexican girls

we were mean and perfect
for what we were
hungover
we could
damn well
do the job

but
it didn't touch us
ever

those filthy peeling walls

the sound of drills and
cutting blades

the sparks

we were some gang
in that death ballet

we were magnificent

we gave them
better than they asked

yet

we gave them
nothing.

all the casualties...

▲▲

I told her then in bed
after flying all the way
down there
I told her in bed
afterwards,
"there's no going back,
you know, it's too god
damned bad . . ."

and it was
although I stayed 2 or
3 days
and then she drove me
to the airport
the dog was in the
back seat
that dog who had lived
with us
those few
years.

I got out
told her
"don't come in,"
the dog jumped up
and down,
he knew I was going,
I roughed him up,
he slobbered across
my face.
what crap.
I leaned in
holding my bag,
she gave me a little
goodbye kiss,
then I turned and
walked into the
airport office

up to the counter
got out the
other half of the round-trip
ticket.

"smoking or non-
smoking?" the clerk
asked.

"drinking," I
said.

I got my boarding pass
and walked toward
the gate
feeling bad

for everybody
I knew

didn't know

would
know.

A Love Poem

▲▲▲

all the women
all their kisses the
different ways they love and
talk and need.

their ears they all have
ears and
throats and dresses
and shoes and
automobiles and ex-
husbands.

mostly
the women are very
warm they remind me of
buttered toast with the butter
melted
in.

there is a look in the
eye: they have been
taken they have been
fooled. I don't quite know what to
do for
them.

I am
a fair cook a good
listener
but I never learned to
dance—I was busy
then with larger things.

but I've enjoyed their different
beds
smoking cigarettes
staring at the
ceilings. I was neither vicious nor

unfair. only
a student.

I know they all have these
feet and barefoot they go across the floor as
I watch their bashful buttocks in the
dark. I know that they like me, some even
love me
but I love very
few.

some give me oranges and vitamin pills;
others talk quietly of
childhood and fathers and
landscapes; some are almost
crazy but none of them are without
meaning; some love
well, others not
so; the best at sex are not always the
best in other
ways; each has limits as I have
limits and we learn
each other
quickly.

all the women all the
women all the
bedrooms
the rugs the
photos the
curtains, it's
something like a church only
at times there's
laughter.

those ears those
arms those
elbows those eyes

looking, the fondness and
the wanting I have been
held I have been
held.

Horsemeat

▲▲

▲▲▲ 1 ▲▲▲

I park, get out, lock the car, it's a perfect day, warm and
easy, I feel all right, I begin walking toward the track
entrance and a little fat guy joins me, he walks at my side,
I don't know where he came from.
"hi," he says, "how you doing?"
"o.k.," I say.
he says, "I guess you don't remember me. you've seen me before,
maybe two or three times."
"maybe so," I say, "I'm at the track every day."
"I come maybe three or four times a month," he says.
"with your wife?" I ask.
"oh no," he says, "I never bring my wife."
we walk along and I walk faster; he struggles to keep up.

"who you like in the first?" he asks.
I tell him that I haven't gotten the Form yet.

"where do you sit?" he asks.
I tell him that I sit in a different place every time.

"that God-damned Gilligan," he says, "is the worst jock
at the track. lost a bundle on him the other day. why
do they use him?"
I tell him Whittingham and Longden think he's all
right.
"sure, they're friends," he answers. "I know something about
Gilligan. want to hear it?"
I tell him to forget it.

we are nearing the newspaper stands near the entrance
and I slant off toward the left as if I were going to buy
a paper.
"good luck," I tell him and drift off.
he appears startled, his eyes go into shock; he reminds me
of some women who only feel secure when somebody's thumb is
up their ass.

36

he looks about, spots a grey-haired old man with a
limp, rushes up, catches stride with the old guy and begins
talking to him . . .

▲▲▲ II ▲▲▲

Being alone has always been very necessary to me. At one time I
was on a hot winning streak at the racetrack. The money just
came to me. A certain basic simple system was working for me.
The horses moved south and I walked off my job and followed
them down to Del Mar.

   It was a good life. I'd win each day at the track. I had a routine.
After the track I'd stop off at the liquor store for my fifth of
whiskey and my six-pack of beer and the cigars. Then I'd get
back into the car and cruise the coast for a motel, park, carry in
my stuff, shower, change clothes and then get my ass back into
the car and cruise the coast again—this time for an eating place.
And what I would look for was an eating place without people in
it. (The worst, I know.) But I didn't like crowds. I always found
one. Went in and ordered.

   So, this particular night, I found a place, went in, sat at the
counter, ordered: porterhouse with french fries, beer. Everything
was fine. The waitress didn't bother me. I sucked at my beer,
ordered another. Then the meal came. God damn, it looked
good. I began. I had a few fine bites, then the door opened and
this fellow came in. There were 14 empty stools at the counter.
This fellow sat down next to *me*.

   "Hi, Doris, how's it going?"

   "O.k., Eddie. How ya doing?"

   "Fine."

   "What'll ya have, Eddie?"

   "Oh, just a coffee, I guess . . . "

   Doris brought Eddie his coffee.

   "I think the fuel pump on my car is going out . . . "

   "Always some damn thing, huh Eddie?"

   "Yeah, now my wife needs new plates, Doris."

   "You mean houseware?"

"I mean mouthware!"

"Oh, Eddie, ha, ha, ha!"

"Well," Eddie said, "when it rains it pours!"

I picked up my plate and my beer, my fork, my knife, my spoon, my napkin, my ass and moved it all over to a far booth. I sat down and began again. As I did I watched Eddie and Doris. They were whispering. Then Doris looked at me:

"Is everything all right, sir?"

"Now," I told her, "it is."

▲▲▲ III ▲▲▲

a fat Mexican woman in front of me in line
lays down her last two dollars all in change:
quarters, dimes and nickles
as she calls the wrong number.
I walk up, bet twenty win and call the
wrong number also as
a fart of thunder erupts in the sky followed
by a distant light
small drops of rain begin their work and we
go out and watch the last race:
12 three-year-olds at a flat mile, non-winners
of two races
they break in a spill of color and chance
fight for position on the quick turn
enter the backstretch before the enchanting
mountains
there's still a chance for everybody
except that the 6 horse snaps a front
foreleg and
tosses a millionaire called Pincay to the
hard hard ground as
some of the poor groan for him
others don't care
and a few are secretly delighted.
the track ambulance circles counter-

clockwise
the race unfolds unfolds
as 3 contenders straighten out for the
stretch drive
the favorite gives way
falls back
as the 2nd favorite and a 26-to-one shot
drive to the wire as a single 8-legged creature,
the last head bob in the photo belonging to
the longshot.
most of us tear up our tickets and begin our
walk toward the parking lot and whatever is
left over for us
the hot drops of rain increase
become cold
all we hope for now is that our automobiles
might still be there
as Pincay regains consciousness in the track
infirmary and asks, "what the hell
happened?"

▲▲▲ IV ▲▲▲

I have a saying, "You will find the lowest of the breed at the racetrack." I am there almost every day working on my various systems, waiting the long 30 minutes between races. I don't know how many of those 30 minute waits I have given away over the years sitting there waiting for a race that is generally over in a minute and nine seconds. And at the quarter horse races most are finished in 17 seconds plus a tick.

A racetrack never has a losing day. For each dollar bet they give back about 84 cents. In Mexico they give back 75 cents. At some of the European tracks they give back 50 cents. It doesn't matter, the people continue to play. Check the faces at any track going into the last race. You will see the story.

When I came out of the Charity Ward of the L.A. County General Hospital in 1955 after drinking ten years without missing a night or a day (except while in jail) they told me that if I ever took another drink I would be dead. I went back to my shack job and I asked her, "What the hell am I going to do now?"

"We'll play the horses," she said.

"Horses?"

"Yeah, they run and you bet on them."

She had found some money on the boulevard. We went out. I had 3 winners, one of them paid over 50 bucks. It seemed very easy.

We went a second time and I won again.

That night I decided that if I mixed some wine with milk that it might not hurt me. I tried a glass, half wine, half milk. I didn't die. The next glass I tried a little less milk and a little more wine. By the time the night was over I was drinking straight wine. In the morning I got up without hemorrhaging. After that I drank *and* played the horses. 27 years later I am still doing both. Time is made to be wasted.

▲▲▲ V ▲▲▲

my women of the past keep trying to locate me.
I duck into dark closets and pull the overcoats
about.

at the racetrack I sit in my clubhouse seat
smoking cigarette after cigarette
watching the horses come out for the post parade
and looking over my shoulder.

I go to bet—this one's ass looks like that one's
ass used to.
I duck away from her.

that one's hair might have her under it.
I get the hell out of the clubhouse and go
to the grandstand to bet.

I don't want a return of any of the past.
I don't want a return of any of those glorious
ladies of my past,
I don't want to try again, I don't want to see
them again even in silhouette;
I gave them all, gave all of them to all the other
men in the world, they can have the darlings,
the tits the asses the thighs the minds
and their mothers and fathers and sisters and
brothers and children and dogs and x-boy friends
and present boy friends, they can have them and
fuck them and hang them
upsidedown.

I was a terrible and a jealous man who mistreated
them and it's best that they are with you
for you will be better to them and I will be
better to myself
and when they phone me or write me or leave
messages
I will send them all to you
my fine fellows

I don't deserve what you have and I want to
keep it that way.

▲▲▲ VI ▲▲▲

got to the track early to study my figures and here's this
man coming by
dusting seats. he keeps at his work, dusting away,
probably glad to have his job.
I'm one of those who doesn't think there is much difference
between an atomic scientist and a man who cleans the crappers
except for the luck of the draw—
parents with enough money to point you toward a more
generous death.

of course, some come through brilliantly, but
there are thousands, millions of others, bottled up, kept
from even the most minute chance to realize their
potential.

"how's it going?" I asked him as he dusted by.

"o.k., how about you?" he asked.

"I do all right on the horses. it's the women where I lose."

he laughed. "yeah. a man can have two or three bad experiences,
it can really set him back."

"I wouldn't mind two or three," I told him. "I've had
eleven or twelve."

"man, you must know something. who do you like in the first?"

I told him that the entry, which was reading 4-to-one should
finish one-two. (45 minutes later it did.) but it wasn't 45
minutes later. he went dusting off and I thought of all the
rotten jobs and how glad I had been to have them. for a
while. then it was always a matter of quitting or getting fired
and both felt good.

when you sleep and live with the same woman for over two
years you know what's finally going to happen only you don't know
why. it's not in the charts. it's in past performance
but it's not in the charts.

my friend, dusting off the track, he didn't know either.

I got up and walked over for a coffee. the girl behind the
counter was a slim brunette with a tiny blue flower in her hair,
nice eyes, nice smile. I paid for my coffee.
"good luck," she said.

"you too," I said.

I took my coffee back to my seat, the wind came from the west,
I took a sip off the top and waited for the action, thinking of
many things, too many things. it just went into the grass and
trees and dirt out there, one mile, the dirty shades in
dirty rooming houses flapping back and forth in a light wind,
torn, the dirty troops entering the new village,
and all my old girl friends unhappy again with their new men.

I sat back and drank my coffee and waited for the first
race.

▲▲▲ VII ▲▲▲

I am at the track
and go up to bet
ten win on the four
horse
somebody hollers,
"HEY!"
I look up.
a teller 3 windows
down is looking
at me and
smiling.
he's a young fellow
in a white shirt
smiling away.
I walk up to him.
"how the hell you
been doing?" he
asks.
"o.k.," I say,
"how's it been
with you?"

"fine," he says
and reaches
out.
we shake hands.
"well," I tell
him, "stay in
there!"
"you too!" he
grins.

I turn and walk
off, thinking,
who was that?

then I see a
young girl with
long legs.
she is wearing a
beret.

unusual.
I follow
her.

▲▲▲ VIII ▲▲▲

I pay my way in, find a seat far from everybody, sit down.
I have seven or eight good quiet minutes, then I hear a
movement: a young man has seated himself near me, not next
to me but one seat away, although there are hundreds of
empty seats elsewhere.
another Mickey Mouse, I think. why do they always need
me?
I keep working at my figures.
then I hear his voice: "Blue Baron will take the first
race."
I make a note to scratch that dog and then I look up and

it seems that this remark is directed to me: there's
nobody else within fifty yards.
I see his face.
he has a face women would love: utterly bland and
blank.
he has remained untouched by circumstance,
a miracle of zero.
even I gaze on him, enchanted:
it's like looking at an endless lake of milk
never rippled by even a pebble.

I look back down at my Form.

"who do you like?" he asks.

"sir," I tell him, "I'd prefer not to talk."

he looks at me from behind his perfectly trimmed black moustache,
there is not one hair longer than the other or out of place;
I've tried moustaches; I've never cared enough for mirrors
to keep something that unnatural.

he says, "my buddy told me about you. he says you don't talk
to anybody."

I get up, take my papers three rows down and sixteen seats
over, I take out my set
of red rubber earplugs, jam them in.

I feel for the lonely, I sense their need, but I also feel
that they should all
comfort each other and leave me alone.

so, plugs in, I miss the flag raising ceremony, being deep
into the Form.

I would like to be human
if they would only let me.

45

I had been up until 3 a.m. the night before.
heavy drinking: beer, vodka, wine
and there I was at the track
on a Sunday.
it was hot.
everybody was there.
the killers, the lovers, the fools.
the brother of Jesus Christ.
the uncle of Mickey Mouse.
there were 50,000 of them.
the track was giving away
free caps
and 45,000 of those people were
wearing caps
and there weren't enough seats
and the crappers were crowded
and during the races
the people screamed so loud
that you couldn't hear
the announcer and
the lines were so long
it took you
20 minutes to lay a bet and
in between running to the crapper
and trying to bet
it was a day you
would rather begin
all over again
someplace else
but it was too late and
there were elbows and assholes every-
where and
all the women looked dumb and ugly and
all the men looked stupid and ugly
and suddenly
I got a vision of

the whole mass of them copulating
in the infield
like death blasting death with
stinking and stale semen.
they were walking all around
belching, farting
bumping into each other
stinking
losing
lost
hating the dream
for not working . . .

▲▲▲ X ▲▲▲

I've been going to the track for years
and tonight between the 6th and 7th races
I was in the men's crapper
at Los Alamitos
and this man walked in with a
corned beef on rye.
he walked up to the urinal
and holding the sandwich with one
hand
he unzipped with the other
got it out
and urinated.
then
having finished
he shook it and zipped-up with
his non-sandwich hand
then stood at the urinal and took
a big bite out of the sandwich
turned
and walked out of there without
washing his hands.

47

I keep telling people that there are
more things to the racetrack than
horses.

▲▲▲ **XI** ▲▲▲

I don't know where they come from . . .
the vet's home, probably . . .
they're old, balding, macho but
sexless.
the sex drive is no longer important,
they are at the track every day
arguing over their choices,
laughing . . .
sometimes between races they'll
talk about sports: which is
the best baseball team, the best
hockey team, the best basketball or
football team, amateurs and
professionals are discussed, and
who's the best player at each
position . . .
they often become angry and shout
at each other.

they wear old clothing, greys and
browns, they wear large shoes and
they each have a wristwatch . . .
and while other men their age
fight each other
in the arena of existence
they sit about and argue about
whether the screen pass is any longer
a valid offensive weapon in professional
football. (I don't think that they are
really interested, there's simply
nothing else to do.)

they bet, first standing in front of the
window, talking, making last minute
adjustments, then one of them bets for
all of them.
the races end, of course, and each
evening they leave . . .
a wavering line of them . . .
some stumbling a bit as if
they were walking on their
shoelaces . . .

they look worn and done,
defeated.

▲▲▲ XII ▲▲▲

ten minutes before post time
the horses, jocks, outriders
come out
for the post parade.
some of the people go to
watch.

usually about six minutes to
post
the parade is over
and here they come:
THE TIDE.

they come sweeping in
toward the betting windows:
little old bent women
cheap hold-up men
the unemployed
the A.F.D.C.
the crippled
the mad

the damned
the dull
the bored
the dull and the bored
the worn
the gimpy
the styleless
the defeated and the driven
the child molesters
the pickpockets
the Food Stampers
the muggers
the wetbacks
the clerk-typists
the wife-beaters
the midgets
the whores
the unemployed air-controllers
the displaced auto workers
the fortune tellers
the glass-blowers
the night watchmen
the female-libbers
the dog catchers on sick leave
members of the city council
private dicks
bank examiners
bit men
hit men
your friends and
mine.

▲▲▲ XIII ▲▲▲

I was out there again today. There are some creatures out there,
shirttails hanging out, shoes run down, eyes dulled. Many are
there day after day. How they manage to keep going is the

mystery. They are losers. But somehow they manage to find the entrance fee, somehow they manage to place feeble bets. But today I saw the worst. I had also seen him the day before. He looked lower, more hopeless than any skid row bum, he had a scabby beard, part of the leather had pulled away from the soles of his shoes, showing his bare feet. He wore a greasy brown overcoat but he had a bit of money. I saw him placing bets. He didn't sit in the stands but on some steps outside where he played a harmonica very badly. I looked at him. He had on glasses but one of the lenses had fallen out and the one that remained was nearly black. As I walked slowly by he started talking to me. He spoke rapidly, "Hey, ge out ree hoo nar bah!" The sentences that followed were of a similar order. I couldn't imagine this man placing a bet or driving an automobile. But he had a right. Who said he couldn't? And who said he had to *look* a certain way? Or talk a certain way? Society dictated modes and ways. He was outside all that. I remembered starving in New York City, trying to be a writer. One night I had gone and bought a bag of popcorn, it was my first food in several days. The popcorn was hot and greasy and salty, each kernel a miracle. I walked along in a beautiful trance, feeling the kernels in my mouth, feeling them enter my body. My trance was not entire. Two large men walked toward me. They were talking to each other. One of them looked up just as they passed me and he said loudly to his buddy, "Jesus Christ, did you see *that?*" I was the freak, the idiot, the one who didn't fit. I walked along, the kernels not tasting quite so good.

As I passed the man at the racetrack sitting on the steps I knew that any of us could get lost forever in the crowd, some of us even wanted to. I walked and found a seat. The horses broke from the gate. It was 6 furlongs. I had the one horse in a maiden race. Orange silks. The one hole is usually bad at 6 furlongs but I had a reason for the bet. My horse broke poorly, rushed, fell back, I lost sight of him, then as they took the curve for home I saw orange silks again, he was coming from the outside. He seemed to hesitate in mid-stretch, then he came on again to win drawing away. They put up the price. $14.60. I had it ten win. $73. I got up to cash my ticket. When I did I no longer saw the

man sitting on the steps. I didn't see him the rest of the day. I'll
be looking for him tomorrow. There's a good card going. Three
maiden races. I love those maiden races.

▲▲▲ **XIV** ▲▲▲

driving in for a wash and
wax with nothing to do but light a cigarette and
stand in the sun . . . no rent, no trouble . . .
hiding from the whores . . .

. . . here it comes, glistening black, you tip the man
50 cents, get in, yank up the aerial, adjust side mirror,
start it, turn the radio classical, steer it out
into the streets . . .

open sun roof, take the slow lane, hangover lessening,
now sleepy in the sun . . . you're there . . .

the parking lot attendants know you: "hey, Champ,
how's it going?"

inside, you open the Form, decide to have a day
with the runners . . . already you've spotted two low-
price sucker bets in the first race that will not
win—that's all you need, an edge . . .

"Hank . . ."

it's somebody behind you, you turn, it's your old
factory buddy, Spencer Bishop.

"hey, Spence . . ."

"hey, man, I hear you been fooling the people, I
hear you been going around to the universities and
giving lectures . . ."

"that's right, my man . . . "

"what are you going to do when they find you out?"

"I'll go back to the factory . . . "

you go to your seat and watch them come out for the
post parade.
you could be painting, or in the botanical gardens . . .
the 6 looks good in the Form *and* in the flesh . . .
7/2 is not the world but it's over a third.

you get up and move toward the windows.
the screenplay is finished, you're into the 4th
novel, the poems keep arriving . . . not much with
the short story but that's waiting, fixing itself
up, that whore is getting ready.

"ten-win-six," you say to the teller.

it's the beginning of a most pleasant afternoon.

my next lecture will be
The Positive Influences
of Gambling
as a Means of
Defining Reality as
Something that
Can Be Touched Like
a Book of Matches or
a Soup Spoon.

yes, you think, going back to sit down,
it's true.

▲▲▲ XV ▲▲▲

some fat son-of-a-bitch with
a large pink pig's head
on his body
came rushing up to me
(why?)
anyhow
I pretended to be looking away
and as he closed in
I dug my elbow into his gut.
I felt it sink in like it was
entering a sack of dirty
laundry.

"mother," he gasped,
"help . . ."

"you all right, buddy?" I
asked.

he looked as if
he was going to puke.
his mouth opened.
he cupped his hands and
a pair of
yellow and green false teeth
with faded pink insides
fell into his palms.

I walked on through the crowd
and found a betting line.
I decided to bet the last 5 races
and leave.
the only way I would stay
would be for $200 an hour
tax free.

54

▲▲▲ XVI ▲▲▲

I have my figures ready for the
6th race
then I look up
and see, well,
there in the stands ahead of
me
a fellow sits upright.
his face is smooth and
bland.
the physiognomy is set at
absolute zero.

he has a yellow pencil.
he flips it over
once
into the air and
catches it with
one hand.

he does it
again

and again

with the same
timing.

what is he
doing?

he just sits there
and continues to
repeat the
maneuver.

I begin to

count:

one two three
four five six . . .

23, 24, 25, 26,
27 . . .

his movements are
dull and graceless,
he reminds me of a
factory machine.

this man is my enemy.

45, 46, 47, 48 . . .

his face has the
taut dead skin
of a mounted
ape

and I am sitting
with my two-day
two-night
hangover
watching . . .

53, 54, 55 . . .

this will be my
life in hell: watching
men like that
sitting forever
tossing and
catching pencils
with one
hand

in that same
non-innovational
rhythm . . .

I am in vertigo.
I feel a pressing
at the temples
as if I was going
mad.

I can't watch
any longer.

I get up and walk
away from the
seating section
as I think,

it will never
let go
with the women
you live with
or wherever you
go, supermarkets,
bazaars, hang-glider
meets, it will
find you, maul you,
piss over you, let
you know
about it
again.
and there will be
nobody
you can talk to
about it.

▲▲▲ XVII ▲▲▲

I lost a dollar at the track today and I know that's
stupid: it's better to win a hundred or lose a hundred—
there is at least the jostle of emotions
but I was 29 bucks ahead going into the last race so I
laid 30 win on this 8-to-one shot going into the last, he
came in second, it was back luck
that's all. so
I lost a dollar.

but sometimes we've got to settle for not very much;
we need our rest; great tragedy or great victory will
arrive soon enough.

so I sit here tonight sipping on my wine and listening to
a Vaughan Williams symphony on the radio
and you too are probably waiting for better or worse.
waiting is the greater portion of being around.

I waited on that 8-to-one shot in the last race and
he came on in the stretch rapidly closing the space
between himself and the horse nearing the wire, he came
with a beautiful rush, pounding and driving, to fall a
head short.

such is the life of a gambler: to go away then and wait
to return.

not all of us are gamblers; those who aren't don't
matter.

▲▲▲ XVIII ▲▲▲

the two old guys behind me were talking.
"look at that 7 horse. he's 35-to-one.
how can he be 35-to-one?"

"yeah, he looks good to me too," says
the other old guy.

"let's bet him."

"o.k., we'll both bet him."

they get up to make their bets.

I've already bet. I've got 40 win
on the 2nd favorite.
I win four days out of five at a
racetrack. It doesn't seem to be
any problem.

I open my newspaper, read the financial
section, get depressed, turn to the front
pages looking for robbery, rape, murder.

the two old men are back.
"look, the 7 horse is 40-to-one now,"
says one of them.

"I can't believe it," says the
other.

the horses are loaded into the gate, the
flag goes up, the bell rings, they break
out.

it's a mile-and-one-sixteenth race, they
take the first turn, go down the backstretch,
circle the last turn, come down the stretch, get
past the finish line.

the 2nd favorite wins by a neck, pays
$7.80. I make $116.00 on that race.

there is silence behind me.
then one of the old men says, "the 7 horse
didn't run at all."

"nope," says the other, "I don't understand
it."

"maybe the jock didn't try," says
his friend.

"that must have been it," says
the other.

like most other men in the world
they believe that their failure
is caused by any and many factors
besides themselves.

I watch the two old guys
gather over their Racing Form
to make their selection in the
next race.

"gee, look at this!" says one of the
old guys, "they got Red Rabbit ten-to-
one on the morning line. he looks better
than the favorite."

"let's bet him," says the other old
guy.

they leave their seats and move toward the
betting windows.

▲▲▲ XIX ▲▲▲

I am sitting in the stands with a
two-night, two-day hangover;
the second night was the worst:
white wine, red wine and
tequila.

I am out here because I have
evolved an astonishing
new theory on
how to beat the races.

the money is secondary:
it only operates as a guideline
to see if I am on
the given path.

I picked up $302
the day before
and I am $265 ahead
going into the sixth.

I can barely function
but the new theory
(Formula K) enacts itself:
M plus S plus C plus O
(brought down to
the relative power of
¼ each):
and the horse with the
lowest total is
the winner.

it is like knowing
one of the secrets
of life itself.
when your figures tell you

61

that a 2nd, 3rd or 4th
favorite
can beat the favorite
and when your figures
select only *one* horse,
it is a very curious and
magic feeling, of course,
and you learn to apply
the same simplicity to
other areas of existence,
but to the spiritual
rather than the mathematical
areas.

▲▲▲ XX ▲▲▲

20 minutes later
I had made my bets
and I walked out to the parking lot
and to my car.
I got in
opened the windows and
took off my shoes.

then I noticed
that I was blocked in.
some guy had parked behind me
in the exit space.

I started my engine
put it in reverse and
jammed my bumper against him.
he had his hand brake on
but luckily he was in neutral and
I slowly ground him back against
another car.
now the other car wouldn't be able

62

to get out.

what made a son-of-a-bitch
that way?
didn't they have any
consideration?

I put my shoes on
got out
and let the air out of his
left front tire.

no good.
he probably had a spare.
so I let the air out of his
left rear tire
got back into my car and
maneuvered it out of there
with some difficulty.

it felt good to
drive out of that racetrack.
it sure as hell felt better than
my first piece of ass and
many of the other pieces
which followed.

60 yard pass

▲▲▲

most people don't do very well and I get discouraged with
their existence, it's such a waste: all those
bodies, all those lives
malfunctioning: lousy quarterbacks, bad waitresses, in-
competent carwash boys and presidents, cowardly
goal-keepers
inept
garage mechanics
bumbling tax accountants and
so forth.

yet

now and then

I see a single performer doing something with a
natural excellence

it

can be
a waitress in some cheap cafe or a 3rd string
quarterback
coming off the bench with 24 seconds on the clock
and completing that winning
60 yard pass.

which lets me believe that
the possibility of the miracle is here with us
almost every day

and I'm glad that now and then
some 3rd string quarterback
shows me the truth of that belief
whether it be in science, art, philosophy,
medicine, politics and / or etc.

else I'd shoot all the lights out of
this fucking city
right now.

a beginning
▲▲

when women stop carrying
mirrors with them
everyplace they go
maybe then
they can talk to me
about
liberation.

jack-knife

▲▲▲

as you see the large
truck and trailer
jack-knifed over
the edge of the freeway
in the evening rain
you notice the red letters
on the side: LUCKY

as your wipers throb and
scrape
you think, I should have
stayed home and worked on
the little drawings for
the next novel

then you feel shame for
such conservatism
hit the throttle and
begin weaving through and
past the other drivers

turning the radio up
to some sexpot singing
about how much she'd
like your love

you glide along
to the end of the
freeway

red light

sitting in the rain
with the others

many of the people probably
listening to the same
sexpot singing how

much she'd like
their love

you think about that
poor guy in the LUCKY
truck
wonder if he'll lose
his job

as the signal changes
and we move onto
the boulevard.

a sad poem

▲▲

I live in a middle class neighborhood of an unfashionable
city
but even here there have been murders a half a block
away
and I would like to write five novels before I leave.
my security system man is a weightlifter and he
walked about the house
checking it out and he noticed the bookcase:
"geez, ya got a lot of books!"
"I write."
"you're a writer?"
"yeah..."
"can I have one of your books?"
I pulled one down and autographed it for him.

he finished the housecheck and recommended various
measures.
I agreed, wrote him a check for the total amount.

the next day he phoned: "listen, I was up all night
reading that book. you've been there: all those
women, the booze... you remind me of myself..."

"thanks."

"what I like about your writing, it's easy to
understand. I'm going to show your book to all
the boys down at the office."

"o.k."

"listen, I saw those weights in your bedroom. do
you lift those weights?"

"no, they're mostly a decoration."

"you ought to work out..."

"I know . . ."

after he hung up I went in and took a pull at the
weights (only 65 pounds), did ten overhead, ten gut
pulls, ten arm lifts.

that was two months ago, I haven't lifted them
since but
we haven't been robbed either.
just more books stolen from the bookcase (many
originals I'll never be able to replace) by
friends who come by to drink my wine and talk and
laugh with me.
no security system will detect that type
except my own
which has always known and which keeps failing
for their sake
which is no way to conduct any type of business,
even this one.

70

playing it out
▲▲

there are only two men I can really
relate to in this world and
one is on his deathbed
and the other, well, his wife
just ran away from him.

and I sit here typing
these things
drunk
as everybody else in the
neighborhood is
asleep except for
two dogs
barking
at the sound of these
keys.

it's strange, I think,
that the best I know are
in trouble
while the worst are
healthy, calm and
prosperous;
they are also exception-
ally dull
and consider themselves
my friends.

I keep typing these
drunk poems
sitting in this chair
smoking too many
cigarettes
and not understanding
anything
and finally
not wanting to.

just drinking and
cracking these keys to
make the dogs
bark
night into morning.

on and off the road

▲▲▲

flying into a strange town, being met at the
airport by a student, then demanding to know
where is the nearest bar

getting the drinks down while waiting for the
luggage
then

being driven to the hotel, first demanding to
be let off at the nearest liquor store

later in the hotel room, switching on the tv,
getting into bed with the bottle, thinking, I
don't have to read until tomorrow night
then

drinking that night away . . .

▲▲▲

on stage with another bottle, insulting them
between poems, they look as if they need the
artistry of the insult,
anyhow

you're going to get your check whether you're
good or bad
and there's always the chance you might end up
in bed with a coed . . .

▲▲▲

flying out of town, back to L.A., your woman
meeting you at the airport, driving you in—
you're a traveling salesman: you sell
poems.

back at the place you try to sober up

get in an argument with your woman
about whether you got laid or not (you
never ask *her*)

she claims you got laid. she's sometimes
wrong.

you will be glad to be at the racetrack
the next day
just being a horseplayer, standing with the
other horseplayers watching them run: that's
the good part: not being a poet, not having to
get under the sheets with a coed and doing it
like you're immortal,
meanwhile

your woman screaming, "the next reading
I'm going with you! *look* at you! they've sucked
you *dry*!"

"gimme another beer, baby . . ."

she just doesn't understand: it's the only job you
have

it's the only thing you can do.

too late

▲▲

I was a slow developer.
I got good too late:
high school was over,
it was summer
with no job
and my father looking
at me over the plates
at mealtime.

during the day I'd
hang around the lots:
"hey, anybody want to
play football? baseball?"

now and then I'd get
a few guys and then
I'd look good:
I could powder the ball
better than anybody,
I could make impossible
graceful catches over my
shoulder.

at football
I was the best broken-
field runner in the
neighborhood—
I laughed at them
while
dodging past
while the young girls
and neighborhood people
applauded my
mastery.

but the guys didn't
want to play
anymore: "listen, Hank,

75

we've got things to
do.
why didn't you
go out for the teams
while you were still
in school?"

then they'd leave
and the people would
leave and I would be
standing in the vacant
lot
alone.

then I'd go
back to the house
and
back to my father
watching me over his
dinner plate:

"well, son, what did you
do today? did you find
a job?"

he should have seen me
with all the young girls
screaming.

he just didn't know
who he was
sitting at the table
with.

on being 20

▲▲

my mother knocked on my roominghouse door
and came in
looked in the dresser drawer:
"Henry you don't have any clean
stockings?
do you change your underwear?"

"Mom, I don't want you poking around in
here . . . "

"I hear that there is a woman
who comes to your room late at
night and she drinks with you, she lives
right down the hall."

"she's all right . . . "

"Henry, you can get a terrible
disease."

"yeah . . . "

"I talked with your landlady, she's a
nice lady, she says you must read a lot
of books in bed because as you fall to sleep at
night the books fall to the floor,
they can hear it all over the
house, heavy books, one at midnight,
another at one a.m., another at 2 a.m.,
another at four."

after she left I took the library books
back
returned to the roominghouse and
put the dirty stockings and the dirty
underwear and the dirty shirts into
the paper suitcase
took the streetcar downtown

77

boarded the Trailways bus to
New Orleans
figuring to arrive with ten dollars
and let them do with me
what they would.

they did.

the troops

▲▲

World War II
I was 21
riding a bus to
New Orleans

there were many
army men
on that
bus

there were only
2
young men
not in
uniform

a red-haired
fellow and
me.

the red-haired
fellow
kept explaining
his
position to the
army
boys:

"Jesus, you've
got to
believe me, I
want to be with
you guys
but I can't
go, I've got a
bad
heart!"

"that's all
right," they
told him.

I didn't need
a
confessional,
I needed a
savior.
I pulled out
my pint,
had a
nip, looked
out the
window . . .

it was
getting into
evening
when the bus
was
stopped
at the edge
of the
desert
by some more
soldiers

some soldiers
stood outside
as 2 entered
the bus

they heavily
trudged
along
nerve-endings
of order and

80

disorder

they asked
each passenger:

"where were
you
born?"

it appeared
that 9-tenths of
the bus
were born in
the
midwest

and when
my turn
came
I said,
"Pasadena,
California."

"where ya
going?"

"funeral, my
brother
died."

they moved
further
down in
the bus

and
came upon
an old

man—

"where were
you
born?"

"I don't
think," the
old man
answered,
"that's any
of your
business."

"Sir, I
asked you,
'where were
you born?' "

"this is a
democracy, I
don't have
to answer
that
question."

"*you son
of a bitch!*"

the soldier
grabbed the
old man
by the
back of
his
coat

lifted him
from his

82

seat

and
they dragged
the
old man
down the
aisle
and out
the
front door
of the
bus.

the bus
stood
there
and we all
looked out
the window
as a group of
soldiers
surrounded
him

we heard:
"we're takin'
you in!"

"but I've
got my
baggage on
the
bus!"

"fuck
your
baggage!"

then a
soldier
motioned
to the bus
driver

the
bus door
closed
and the bus
drove
off.

evening
quickly became
night
everybody was
silent for a
while

then the red-
haired
fellow
started it
up
again:

"listen, I
really want
to go
to this
war, I'd
just give
anything if
I didn't have
this
bad
heart."

84

the bus
just kept on
going.

hog

▲▲

he couldn't get the puck into the net.
he was too slow.
all he was was a hog.
when somebody
on the other team
started busting ass and
ribcage
we'd send him in with instructions to
hammer the fucker out.
the hog would skate in
grinning through his yellow teeth
useful at last.
he was just like death
zeroing in on target:
five minutes later
there would be a man down:
rammed, sticked, sliced
out for the game
maybe the season
and the hog would be sitting in
the penalty box, grinning, his
job done.

nobody liked him.
even in the locker room afterwards
we didn't talk much to him.
he knew.
I mean, we spoke to him.
sometimes even one of the guys
would joke with him about
his night's work
but nobody laughed very
much.

afterwards his wife would be
waiting outside in an old green
station wagon,
a ridiculous battered

machine
and he'd climb in and they'd drive
off
with her at the wheel, a
very tall woman, with a big head,
the car going off as always with
only the right taillight working.

he knew his job.

the walls
▲▲▲

after you've hit the bars a while
drinking
going back to your room with a
fat mama
doing it
sleeping
to awaken in the morning
to find your wallet gone
again

no job
no food
no rent

just a hangover and
the dark peeling walls.

after you've hit the bars a while
you carry your wallet in a front
pocket
you carry a blade
you carry most of your bills
in your shoe

you go to the crapper to make a
withdrawal.

it gets so *ingrained* that
even when you go to your room
alone
you automatically hide
your wallet and your money
and upon awakening
you spend hours
searching . . .

it gets so *ingrained*
that often when you're drinking with

a woman you trust
one who is living with you
you often awaken to tell
her: "shit! I can't find my
wallet!"

"now you know it's here," she
says, "you've just hidden it
somewhere."

and after some hours
you find it.

in the old days there were some
strange times:
once going into a library to
return some books
you stopped the librarian just as
she was taking the books away:
"just a moment, please . . . "
(you saw an edge of green)
and you opened the book and
pulled out 3 twenties and
a ten.

another time
in a Texas roominghouse
after a night of ferocious drinking
the next morning
you found your wallet
but not the money.

the rent was due
and you told the landlady you had
lost your money somewhere . . .

coming in after a sad walk
in the streets

the landlady met you

she had a handful of green
and said,
"Mr. Chinaski, I was vacuuming
your room and the vacuum kept hitting
a bump in the rug and I pulled
the rug back
and there it was . . . "

an honest lovely lady.

luckily, after that, I met more
honest, lovely ladies
some who even put money *in*
my wallet
so I'm not a misogynist
being only two or three hundred
dollars out,
but I have special reservations
about those fat mamas of the streets
because I think the unkindest
crime of all is when
the poor rob the poor
after talking and drinking and
laughing and making love
one leaving the other
broke and hungover
to awaken like that
in some strange city
alone
within dark and
peeling walls.

writing is a state of trance
▲▲▲

she walks in while
I'm typing.

"listen," she says, "I . . . "

as I scream and leap out of
my chair.

"sorry," she says, "I wanted to
ask you about something . . . "

"yes, what is it?"

she leaves and I rip the paper
from the typer and throw it
into the trash.
there's no way of
getting it back.

then I forget about her
start again
am three or four pages
into it when she
walks in,

"listen, I . . . "

"HOLY SHIT!" I leap out of
my chair.

I answer her question and
she leaves.

I sit staring at the page
trying to pick up the flow. it's
gone.
I rip it from the machine,
trash it.

I sit looking at a
cigar box.
White Owl, it says.
over in a corner
I see a dirty bottle.
HYDROGEN PEROXIDE,
it says.

there's nothing like
bitching about
bad luck: I do it
very well.

Dagwood and Blondie

▲▲

I swept underneath and got him
from the rear—
a burst of tracers and
his gas tank exploded.
I saw him trying to
climb out of his
cockpit
but he couldn't
eject himself—
the ball of trailing flame
twisted away
to the right
down and
down
to splash into the
ocean.

I circled over:
nothing left.

when you get into
something like that
somebody has
to win.

I put her back on course
to the base.

well, he had gotten
the one thing done
that everybody
has to do.

I still had
it
to do.

I liked certain

93

delays,
though.

meanwhile, it was a
startling
beautiful day.

Ginsberg?

▲▲

I am sitting in the clubhouse
grandstand
$311 ahead going into the
7th
when this very young man
walks up
stands there
as I am going over the
Form.

"pardon me," he says.

"yes?"

"listen," he says, "I think
I know you . . . "

"no," I say, "you don't."

"don't you know Allen
Ginsberg?"

"I don't know any
Ginsberg . . . "

"didn't you give a
reading at a
nightclub called the
Sweetwater?"

"I don't know what a
reading is . . . "

"listen," he says, "I
know you!"

I stand up and face
him.

"listen, buddy, I'm a
gardener for some
rich people.
that's how I
make it."

I turn and walk off
down through the rows
of seats
feeling good
just like a gardener
should
out on a gambling night
after a row with
his woman.

she said:

▲▲

what are you doing with all those paper
napkins in your car?
we don't have napkins like
that
how come your car radio is
always tuned to some
rock and roll
station?
do you drive around with
some
young thing?

you're
dripping tangerine
juice
on the floor.
whenever you go into
the kitchen
this towel gets
wet and dirty.
why is
that?

when you let my
bathwater run
you never
clean the
tub first.

why don't you
put your toothbrush
back
in the rack?

you should always
dry your
razor.

sometimes I think
you hate
my cat.

Martha says
you were
downstairs
sitting with her
and you
had your
pants off.

you shouldn't wear
those
$100 shoes in
the garden

and you don't keep
track
of what you
plant out there

that's
dumb

you must always
set the cat's bowl back
in
the same place.

don't
bake fish
in a frying
pan . . .

I never saw
anybody
harder on the

98

brakes of their
car
than you.

let's go
to a
movie.

listen what's
wrong with you?
you act
depressed.

oh, yes

▲▲

there are worse things than
being alone
but it often takes decades
to realize this
and most often
when you do
it's too late
and there's nothing worse
than
too late.

the sword
▲▲

watching a tv show
late at night
there's this
Chinese
he's very good
with the sword
he chops off
heads
or
rams it straight
on through or
slices
throats

blood spurts
heads roll like
egg rolls

the movie was
made in
the Orient

therefore
believable
.

I smoke and
drink
in the dark

thinking

my head is
still
on

as
this man

kills 6 or
7 men in 3
minutes

as I sit
and watch

not even
in sorrow for
the murdered

for
what is
important

is that a man
do his
work
well

of course
what is
not important
is necessary
too

often
they are
the same thing:
the important and
the non-
important

my head is
still
on

I pour a

drink
into
it

and

continue
to watch
the movie:

each man
alone
forever.

practice
▲▲

thinking more and more
about death
Christ, it's getting worse
than the horses
but
something
to muse about.

I remember Henry Miller on
the Tom Snyder Show
and Tom asked Henry (who was
very very old then):
"Mr. Miller, do you ever
think of death?"

and he answered simply, "of course,
I do."

I remember reading
an excellent poem about death
by D.H. Lawrence:
"build then
the ship of Death
for you must take
the longest
journey
to
oblivion."

the Christians make a similar
claim.
the other day on the freeway
I was following a car and
the bumper sticker said:
DON'T DIE WITHOUT
JESUS.

then you get

macho guys
in factories and
in the bars
who say:
"the only way to die is
while
you're fucking."

well, I've done that too

any number
of times.

promenade
▲▲▲

I am taking a walk about 2:30 p.m.
pass a group of kids standing around
looking at the engine of a car.
the hood is up and one of them appears
to be working on the motor.

I walk by
am thirty or forty feet away from them
when one of the kids yells:
"hey, old man!"

I stop and turn, wait.
they don't say anything, look down
at the engine.

I wait a moment longer, then turn
and walk along.

I hear one of them laugh, "I don't think
he liked that!"

I don't mind at all: at the age of 62
I can still kick their ass
or
drink any of them under the
table.

close to the grave be damned, there's
not one of them
I'd prefer to be.

it's a good afternoon.

I hope they fix their
engine.

night on a Visa card

▲▲▲

I finished my wine
poured another
took a hit of that
lit a cigarette.

the motel room was
paid for until eleven
a.m.
nice tiny little white
towels
in the bathroom and
the paper-wrapped
soap bars
the celluloid glasses
and the
paper-wrapping over
the toilet seat.

I switched on the
tv
an old black and
white

I left the sound
off and
watched the
faces.
one man and
one woman.
there seemed to
be trouble.
they looked
unhappy although
to most people
their faces would
seem beautiful.

I kept watching

107

them while I smoked
and drank more
wine.

then I shut the
tv off
got out of my
shorts
walked over to
the bed
pulled the cover
and sheet
back
crawled in.

outside on Sunset Boulevard
I could see all the
neon through the
blinds.

I got up
cut the blinds
got back in.
it was good and
dark.
perfect.

there was a tap
on the door.
I opened it with
the chain
on and
looked out.

she was back.
I let her
in.

"it was awful,"
she said
getting un-
dressed.
"some son of a
bitch tried to
rape me and take
my purse in the
parking lot!
I kicked him in
the balls!
compared to *him*
you look
good!"

"thank you,
Sherrie, I feel
blessed..."

she climbed into
bed next to
me.

"I just want to
get off the fucking
streets!"

"yeah. I know what
you mean."

"anything on tv?"
she asked
splashing wine into
her glass.

"just one station,"
I said

getting up and
turning the set on
again
with sound
and returned to the
bed.

the woman on tv
said to the man
on tv, "you've got
to choose between your
wife and me! I'm
tired of hiding what
we are doing!
I want our love to be out
front
like a marching band
like a flag of
glory!"

the man bowed his
head and
didn't answer.

the one
next to me
in bed:
I refilled her
glass.

by eleven a.m. we'd
both be gone
somewhere
else
and the motel maid
would come in and
clean up
after us.

110

she'd go back to
the streets and I'd
go back to
sometimes
writing about
them.

but meanwhile
we sat up on our
butts
pillows to our
backs
the ashtray
between us on
the bed

we drank our wine
from plastic glasses.
it was a
terrible movie
but it was
nice
sitting there in
the dark
watching it
while
smoking and
drinking
without having
to say
anything.

I fall into it
without trying...

▲▲▲

she confessed to me
what made her
do it:

"when I first walked
into your place
I looked around
and it was filthy
but you were the first
man I'd ever met
who didn't have a
tv set,
and it was right
then
that I decided to
fuck you."

of course, what I
didn't like about
that was
somebody else
deciding
anything

so I went out
and bought a second
hand
black and white for
$75

but she still climbed
into bed
with me

so I went out
and purchased a large
screen

color tv with
touch control
and she still climbed
into bed
with me

but we played only the
radio
ate sandwiches in the
park
met all her sisters
and waited for it
to end.

good time girl
▲▲▲

you had *your* crowd
out back . . . your people just
sitting there and drinking and
listening to you . . .

you were *competing* with
me!
but *we* danced!
we had a *good* time!
and god, we *laughed* too!
you missed *Culpepper!*
god, Culpepper was *funny!*
we danced and laughed, that's what
a party's *for!*

you don't know it, but I went back
there
and I saw you with 3 or 4
people,
god, how *somber* you all were!
it was like a meeting of the
dead!

well, you *tried* to compete with me
and you *failed!*
I'm from the country and we know
how to party!
you think I dance too sexy!
sure I shake my ass!
it feels *good!*
WHAT DO YOU WANT ME TO DO, COVER
ALL THIS WITH A GRANNY DRESS?

I dance close and I follow the man's
lead, I was always taught to follow
the man's lead since I was a
little girl!
in the country, that's natural,

there's nothing *dirty* about it!
you're the one with the dirty
mind!
you're *jealous* because you can't
dance.
and you don't *like* people because
you're *afraid* of them!
I *like* people and I *like* parties
and I like to *dance!*
and so do all my sisters, they'd
drive 2,000 miles to go to a
party!

well, why don't you *say* something?
you just sit there drinking and
looking at me!

hey, where the hell are you
going?

you're always running out the
door and jumping into your car
and driving off!

well, if you don't want my
pussy
somebody else
will!

*you don't know nothin' about
parties, you son of a
bitch!*

115

the lady poet

▲▲▲

it was 7 or 8 years ago
we lived together
with our 2 typewriters
working away
and her 2 children
manipulating the room.

she was difficult with
her brats:
"get *away*! can't you see
that Mama is
typing?"

so they would come to me
and I would
answer their questions be-
tween my beers and
my lines.

I really wasn't *too* fond
of them
but I wanted the lady to
do well:
poetry was important to
her,
she became very excited
and hammered the keys
as if great verse
was being drilled
into the page.

when she finished a poem
she'd bring it to me
and I'd read it,
"yes, it's good . . . but
don't you think it'd
read better if you
began at line

4, dropped line
7 . . . and then, of
course, you are going
to need an ending
line, I don't like the
ending . . . "

"what do you think
the ending should
be?"

"how about . . . " and
I would suggest a
line.

"why, yes, of course!"
she'd say, then run over
and reshape the
poem.

▲▲▲

the lady's poems began to
appear in some of the
little magazines
and soon
she was invited to give
readings at the
local poetry holes
and I went with her
and
listened

she had long hair and
wild, wild eyes, and
she danced and pranced up
there with her poems,
overdramatizing,

but she had a great
body
and she
twisted
it
and read and waved her
poems

and the men loved her,
such men as there are in
such places
with their little rhymers
tucked into their
knapsacks
and their neutered faces
glistening—
the applause made the lady
think
that things were really
occurring
and it kept her
twisting
prancing, dancing
and
typing . . .

the lady
one night
after lovemaking
told me,
"some day I will be
greater than
you!"

"at many things,"
I replied, "you
already are."

118

we typed together
and apart
for some years
and as such things finally go
it went.

she dissolved to some
desert town
and I repaired to
East Hollywood
where I lived with some
ladies
who didn't give a fuck
about typing at
all, who really didn't
give a fuck about
anything.

I lived through that time,
got away,
moved to a small town
near the harbor
where I began to hear from
the lady poet
again
via phone and letter.
mainly, I was evasive, having
learned some time ago that
going back
doesn't mesh with going
forward.

"you were my *muse*,"
she said, again and
again, "I can't write
anymore . . ."

so, you see, I served a

purpose:
and that's
a rather nice thing, don't you
think?

much better, I think, than
being known for being kindly
under stress
or having a big throbbing
dick
waving
forevermore ready
to enter those hungry
thighs
where no man, beast or
god
can stay forever
or even
wants to?

space creatures
▲▲▲

they are at the track every
Saturday afternoon: two
immensely fat men
a fat woman
and the fat woman's son
(who is also getting obese
and is the son of one of
the men).

they sit together
eat hotdogs
drink beer
and scream together
during the race
and after the
race.
no matter
who wins
they scream.
between races they
argue while consuming
hotdogs and beer.

I sit and watch them
from a distance.
they are far more
interesting than
the horses or
the war in
Nicaragua.

as I watch
the fattest man
lifts his beercup
(large size)
and gulps down a
mass of suds.
his mouth is

strangely small and
he bites at
the cup and
much of the beer
spills out
runs down
each side
of his chin and
onto
his shirt.
he pulls the cup
out of his mouth
and screams:
"SHIT!"

"YOU ASSHOLE!"
the fat woman
screams at
him.

"SHUT UP!"
he screams
back at her.

then they both
sit there
not angry
at all
as if nothing
had occurred.

then
the other
fat man
says:
"I'M GONNA BET
THE 6, THE 3 AND
THE 9!"

even though
he's only speaking
it's as if
the average person were
shouting.

the son
is dressed in
red pants
white t-shirt
white tennis
shoes.

the two men
are dressed
in black pants
white t-shirts
and very shiny
black shoes.

they look like
brothers.

the woman is
dressed in a
soiled white
dress
wears faded
green
tennis shoes
without socks.

as I watch she
lifts
her beercup
(large size).
she also has
a tiny

mouth
but she has
pinched the edge
of the cup,
made a little
runway.

she drains the
cup
crushes it
flips it off to
one side
belches:
"WHO'S GONNA BUY
THE NEXT FUCKING
ROUND?"

nobody sits
near them.

these,
I think, could be
space creatures
from a distant
planet.

I rather
like them.
their attention span
is limited
but they make
few pretenses.

"I'M GOING TO GARDENA
TONIGHT!" says the man
who isn't *quite* as fat
as the other.

"YOU CAN'T BEAT THOSE
GRAND-
MOTHERS!" says the
fattest.
"THEY SIT ON THEIR
HANDS."

"SHUT UP!"
says
the woman.

the son
in the red pants
never says
anything.
he just sits
around and
stands around
gradually getting
bigger.

then the horses
appear on the track
for the
post parade.

"SHOEMAKER THE
FAKER!" the fattest
man screams at
the world's
winningest
jock.

Shoemaker blinks but
carries on.
having made a
few million

he understands the
rancor of
losers.

then the woman
leaps up.
well, she doesn't
leap . . . she
rises, a
mountain of
womanhood and
says: "HEY, DIDJA
SEE THAT? THE 5
HORSE JUST SHIT!
HE'S GONNA BE
LIGHTER! THAT GIVES
HIM THE ADVANTAGE!
25 TO ONE! I GOT
MY GOD DAMNED
BET!"

"SIT DOWN!" says the
fattest one. "YOU'RE
BLOCKING OUT THE
SUN!"

I leave then.
go to the betting
window.
I bet Shoemaker the
faker.

when I come back
they're gone.
I don't understand
it.

the race goes

126

off.
Shoemaker comes
in at
5 to one.
I've got him
20 win.

they don't
return
after that
race or the
next.

and I realize
that
they are
gone

I am beset with
an inescapable
sadness

they have gone
somewhere

they are somewhere
else

they are drinking
beer and eating

getting bigger
and louder

these
terrible
obnoxious
undefeated

beings.

I miss them.

**upon first reading the immortal
literature of the world—**
▲▲

the school children
bang closed
their heavy
books

and run
ever so gladly
to the
yard

or

even more
alarming—

back to
their
horrible
homes.

there is nothing so
boring
as
immortality.

the history of a tough motherfucker
▲▲

he came to the door one night wet thin beaten and
terrorized
a white cross-eyed tailless cat
I took him in and fed him and he stayed
grew to trust me until a friend drove up the driveway
and ran him over
I took what was left to a vet who said, "not much
chance... give him these pills... his backbone
is crushed, but it was crushed before and somehow
mended, if he lives he'll never walk, look at
these x-rays, he's been shot, look here, the pellets
are still there... also, he once had a tail, somebody
cut it off... "

I took the cat back, it was a hot summer, one of the
hottest in decades, I put him on the bathroom
floor, gave him water and pills, he wouldn't eat, he
wouldn't touch the water, I dipped my finger into it
and wet his mouth and I talked to him, I didn't go any-
where, I put in a lot of bathroom time and talked to
him and gently touched him and he looked back at
me with those pale blue crossed eyes and as the days went
by he made his first move
dragging himself forward by his front legs
(the rear ones wouldn't work)
he made it to the litter box
crawled over and in,
it was like the trumpet of possible victory
blowing in that bathroom and into the city, I
related to that cat—I'd had it bad, not that
bad but bad enough...

one morning he got up, stood up, fell back down and
just looked at me.

"you can make it," I said to him.

he kept trying, getting up and falling down, finally

he walked a few steps, he was like a drunk, the
rear legs just didn't want to do it and he fell again, rested,
then got up.

you know the rest: now he's better than ever, cross-eyed,
almost toothless, but the grace is back, and that look in
his eyes never left . . .

and now sometimes I'm interviewed, they want to hear about
life and literature and I get drunk and hold up my cross-eyed,
shot, runover de-tailed cat and I say, "look, look
at *this*!"

but they don't understand, they say something like, "you
say you've been influenced by Celine?"

"no," I hold the cat up, "by what happens, by
things like this, by this, by *this*!"

I shake the cat, hold him up in
the smoky and drunken light, he's relaxed he knows . . .

it's then that the interviews end
although I am proud sometimes when I see the pictures
later and there I am and there is the cat and we are photo-
graphed together.

he too knows it's bullshit but that somehow it all helps.

131

our curious position

▲▲

Saroyan on his deathbed said,
"I thought I would never die . . . "

I know what he meant:
I think of myself forever
rolling a cart through a
supermarket
looking for onions, potatoes
and bread
while watching the misshapen
and droll ladies push
by.
I think of myself forever
driving the freeway
looking through a dirty
windshield with the radio tuned to
something I don't want
to hear.
I think of myself forever
tilted back in a
dentist's chair
mouth
crocodiled open
musing that
I'm in
Who's Who in America.
I think of myself forever
in a room with a depressed
and unhappy woman.
I think of myself forever
in the bathtub
farting underwater
watching the bubbles
and feeling proud.

but dead, no . . .
blood pin-pointed out of
the nostrils,

my head cracking across
the desk
my fingers grabbing at
dark space . . .
impossible . . .

I think of myself forever
sitting upon the edge
of the bed
in my shorts with
toenail clippers
cracking off
huge ugly chunks
of nail
as I smile
while my white cat
sits in the window
looking out over the
town
as the telephone
rings . . .

in between the
punctuating
agonies
life is such a
gentle habit:
I understand what
Saroyan
meant:

I think of myself forever
walking down the
stairs
opening the door
walking to the
mailbox
and finding all that

133

advertising
which
I don't believe
either.

the sickness
▲▲▲

if
one night
I write
what I consider to
be
5 or 6 good poems
then I begin
to worry:

suppose the house
burns down?

I'm not worried
about
the house
I'm worried
about
those 5 or 6
poems
burning
up

or

an x-girlfriend
getting in
here
while I'm away
and stealing or
destroying
the poems.

after writing
5 or 6 poems
I am fairly
drunk
and
I sit

having a few
more
drinks
while deciding
where to hide
the poems.

sometimes I
hide the poems
while
thinking about
hiding
them
and when I
decide to
hide them
I can't find
them . . .

then
begins the
search

and the
whole room is
a mass of
papers
anyhow

and

I'm very clever
at
hiding poems
perhaps more
clever than I
am
at

writing
them.

so
then
I find them
have another
drink

hide them
again

forget it
then
go
to sleep . . .

to awaken in
late morning
to remember
the poems
and
begin the
search
again . . .

usually only a
ten or fifteen
minute
period of
agony

to find
them
and read
them
and then
not like them

very much

but you know
after all
that
work

all that
drinking
hiding
searching
finding

I decide
it's only
fair
to send
them
out
as a
record of
my travail

which
if accepted
will appear in
a little
magazine
circulation
between
100 and
750

a year-and
one-half
later

maybe.

it's
worth
it.

an old buddy
▲▲

he writes to the editors
telling them that
I'm finished
and encloses masses
of his manuscript
which
when returned
goads him into
vitriolic
response.

it's possible,
of course,
that I'm
finished;
one gets
finished
one way or
the
other.

I think he's
a pretty good
writer
but I wish
he'd go about
submitting his work
without trumpeting
that I'm
dead and done.

class under duress
often creates a
strange and lucky kind
of nobility

as I used to
try to tell him

when I finally
got a chance to
talk

as we drank
together
in the old
days

when
we were both
failed
writers.

take it

▲▲

got it down so tight the hinges squeaked.
threw out all three cats
drove over the two bridges
picked up $414.00 at the harness races
came in
listened to Shostakovitch's First
then finally
cleaned the ring out of the bathtub
filled it
bathed while drinking a bottle of
chilled white wine
then
toweled off
got into bed
legs pointed east
I
inhaled
then
let it out:
the pain and defeat
of the world.
then I
slept like a baby
with big fat balls and
silver hair.

John Dillinger marches on

▲▲▲

I sometimes write about the 30's because
they were a good training ground.
people learned to live with adversity
as a common everyday thing
when trouble came
they adjusted and made the next move,
and if there wasn't one
they often created
one.

and the people who *had* jobs
did them with artistry.
a garage mechanic could *fix* your
car.
doctors made house calls.
cab drivers not only knew every
street in town
but they were also versed in
philosophy.
pharmacists would walk up to you
in drugstores and ask you what you
needed.
the ushers in movie houses were more
handsome than the movie
stars.
people made their own clothes,
repaired their own shoes.
almost everybody did things well.

now people in and out of their
professions are totally
inept,
how they even wipe their own asses
is beyond me.
and when adversity arrives they are
dismayed,
they quit,
spit it out,

143

lay down.
these, coddled to the extremes
are only used to victory or
the soft way.

it's not their fault, I suppose,
that they didn't live
through the 30's
but I'm still hardly tempted to
adore
them.

terminology

▲▲

my other favorite cat seemed to be dying and
I had him in and out of the vet's
for x-rays, consultations, injections,
operations

"anything at all," I told the doc,
"let's try to keep him going ... "

one morning I drove over to pick him
up and the girl at the counter
a vast girl in a wrap-around white
nurse's outfit
asked me, "do you want your cat put
to sleep?"

"what?" I asked.

she repeated her
statement.

"put to sleep?" I asked, "you mean
exterminated ?"

"well, yes," she said, smiling with her
tiny eyes, then looking at the card
in her hand she said, "oh, I see it was
Mrs. Evans who wanted it done ... "

"really?" I asked.

"sorry," she said and walked into the other
room with her card and her sorry fat ass and
her sorry walk and her sorry life and
her sorry death and her sorry Mrs. Evans and
both of their sorry fat shits.

I walked over, sat down and opened up a
cat magazine, then closed it, thinking, it's

just her job, it's something she does, *she* doesn't
kill the cats.

when she came into the office again she no
longer quite disgusted me and I opened the pages
of the cat magazine again and looked at and turned
the pages as if I had forgotten everything, which
I hadn't
exactly.

the star

▲▲▲

I was drunk and they
got me out of my car
put the bracelets on
and made me lay down
on the roadway
in the rain.

they stood in their
yellow raincoats
cops from 3
squadcars.

the water soaked
into my clothing.
I looked up
at the moon through
the raindrops,
thinking,
here I am
62 years old
and being
protected
from myself
again.

earlier that night
I had attended the
opening
of a movie
which portrayed the
life of a drunken
poet:
me.

this then was
my critical review
of their
effort.

the day the epileptic spoke

▲▲▲

the other day
I'm out at the track
betting Early Bird
(that's when you bet at the
track before it opens)
I am sitting there having
a coffee and going over
the Form
and this guy slides toward
me—
his body is twisted
his head shakes
his eyes are out of
focus
there is spittle upon his
lips

he manages to get close to
me and asks,
"pardon me, sir, but could you
tell me the number of
Lady of Dawn in the
first race?"

"it's the 7 horse,"
I tell him.

"thank you, sir,"
he says.

that night
or the next morning
really:
12:04 a.m.
Los Alamitos Quarter Horse
Results on radio
KLAC
the man told me

Lady of Dawn
won the first at
$79.80

that was two weeks
ago
and I've been there
every racing day since
and I haven't seen that
poor epileptic fellow
again.

the gods have ways of
telling you things
when you think you know
a lot

or worse—

when you think
you know
just a
little.

the condition

▲▲▲

all up and down the avenues
the people are in pain;
they sleep in pain, they awaken
in pain;
even the buildings are in pain,
the bridges
the flowers are in pain
and there is no release—
pain sits
pain floats
pain waits
pain is.

don't ask why there are
drunks
drug addicts
suicides

the music is bad
and the love
and the script:

this place now
as I type this

or as you read this:
your place now.

bravo

▲▲▲

summertime dogs
crushed on freeways
as young bodies leap into the
sea
outside rented motels at
Del Mar
as the 4th race unfolds:
a race for
2-year-olds
non-winners
they take the short turn
home
as I stand with
weary
potbelly
fighting the eternal
pattern
light and darkness
spitting
from everywhere

the dogs will die here and
in Normandy

the heart will be held high
like a flag
and potted through the middle
like a cooked
apple

if we can find a band
*let the music
play.*

151

a note to the boys in the back room:

▲▲

I get more and more mimeo chapbooks in the mail
written by fellows who used to know me
in the good old days.

these fellows are all writers
and they write about me
and they seem to remember
what I said
what I did.

some of it is exaggerated
some of it is humorous
and a majority of it is
self-serving—

where I tend to look bad or
ridiculous
or even insane
they always describe themselves
as calm and dependable observers
instead of
(in many cases)
as the non-talented
boring
ass-sucking
pretentious and
time-consuming
little farts
that they were.

I feel no rancor at what they
write.
it's only that I've already done a
better job
with that particular subject
matter

and I would suggest that they

move on to the next man
just as my women have
done.

153

sardines in striped dresses

▲▲▲

all right, they're playing Beethoven again; when I was
sleeping on that park bench in Texas they were playing
Beethoven, when it rained last Sunday and the pier fell
into the water they were playing Beethoven; I walked on
that pier 55 years ago and now it's down in the ocean,
like Atlantis
but things break and vanish, that's not news, got a
letter today from Louise, she says she's leaving the
French Quarter and moving in with her sister in a small
town 45 minutes out of New Orleans.
people are getting tired, people are falling down and getting
back up, and they are playing Beethoven as the bums stop
me outside the post office: "Good morning, sir, have you
got a dollar?"

the old aerial circus is falling from the sky, dogs and
cats look at me oddly, the Klan appears, vanishes, Hitler
sniffles underground between palm tree roots, this cheap
cigar I'm smoking, it says Cuba, it says Havana, smuggled
all this way to gag me as
they are playing Beethoven, as Beethoven plays
William Saroyan is dead Celine is dead but Fante won't
die
legs chopped off, and blind in his narrow grave he won't
die:
3 years laying flat like that in that hospital, what is
he thinking?

I want to go quick like a seedless olive into the mouth
of a fool, as young girls keep arriving from Des
Moines wiggling like sardines in striped dresses, what
does it mean, listening to Beethoven now?

and now it's over . . . "Head for some Palm Springs sun,"
the announcer begins as I tune him out and grimace at
this cigar, turn the radio back up: it's
Mahler, the 10th, right after the Bee's 5th, some hell
of a heavy night as pretty much alone here

154

I think of how much I like Somerset Maugham's title *The Razor's Edge*,
then I put out the fucking cigar, drain some wine,
get up, thinking, it's the
same for everybody, more or less, some more, some
less, Celine's dead, Beethoven's quiet a moment:
it's been a world full of the brave
and I love them all
as outside the
Vincent Thomas Bridge arcs in the dark
holding, just now, the luck of us all.

result

▲▲▲

the room was small but neat and when I visited him
he was on that bed like a grounded seal
and it was embarrassing, I mean,
coming across with the conversation;
I really didn't know him that well
except through his writing,
and they kept him drugged—
they kept operating, chopping parts of him
away
but being a true writer
Fante talked about his next novel.

blind, and cut away, again and again,
he had already dictated one novel
from that bed
a good work, it had been published
and now he talked to me about another
but I knew he wouldn't make it
and the nurses knew
everybody knew
but he just went on talking to me
about his next novel.
he had an unusual plot idea
and I told him it sounded
great,
and after another visit or two
his wife phoned me one afternoon
and told me that
it was over...

it's all right, John, nobody has ever
written that last one.

you were really tough on those nurses, though,
and that pleased me, the way you brought them
running in there in their crinkled whites,
you proved me more than right:
my assertion

that your power of command
with simple language was
one of the magnificent things of
our century.

suggestion for an arrangement

▲▲

it would be nice to die at the typer instead of with my
ass stuck into some hard bed pan.

I visited a writer friend in the hospital who was dying
inch by inch
in the most terrible way
possible.
yet during each visit
(when conscious) he continued to
talk to me
about his
writing (not as an accomplishment but
as a magic obsession)
and he didn't mind my
visits because
he knew I understood exactly what he was
saying.

at his funeral
I expected him to rise from his
coffin and say, "Chinaski,
it was a good run, well
worth it."

he never knew what I looked like
because before I met him
he had become blind
but he knew I
understood
his slow and terrible
death.

I told him one time that
the gods were punishing him because
he wrote so
well.

I hope that I never write that

well, I want to die with my head down on this
machine
3 lines from the bottom of the
page
burnt-out cigarette in my
fingers, radio still
playing

I just want to write
just well enough to
end like
that.

the miracle is the shortest time
▲▲

you know
it was very good
it was
better than
anything

it was like
something
we could
pick up
hold
look at
and then laugh
about.

we were on the
moon
we were *in* the
god damned moon,
we had it

we were in the garden
we were in the
endless pit

never such a place
as that

it was deep
and
it was light
and
it was high

it got so near
to insanity
we laughed so
hard

160

your laughter
and
mine

I remember when
your eyes
said love
loudly

now
as these walls
so quietly
shift.

transformation and disfiguration

▲▲

there were always little tragedies
we heard about them on the job
sitting on those stools
eleven-and-one-half hours a night
every bit of outside news
was greeted by us
much like the inmates of a prison camp

every now and then
a courier would come by and say
"it's 3 to 2, end of the 3rd . . . "

he never said 3 to 2 *who*
because
we were able to decipher all that

one night I heard two fellows
talking:
"Ralph checked out early
when he walked into his house
it was dark
his wife and her lover were in bed
they thought he was a burglar
the lover had a gun
and he shot Ralph . . . "

"where's Louie?"
I asked one night
I hadn't seen Louie
in a couple of weeks
Louie had two jobs
when he slept I didn't know

"Louie?
Louie fell asleep in bed
smoking a cigarette
the mattress caught fire
he burned to death . . . "

162

there were many deaths
among the mail clerks

feeling like an
inmate of a prison
I also felt as if we were
front line troops
under continual bombardment and
attack

when there weren't deaths
there were breakdowns—
people who after years of
sticking letters
just couldn't do it anymore

or there were dismissals
for the slightest reason

it was death and transformation
and disfiguration:
people found
they couldn't walk anymore
or they suddenly
came up with speech defects
or they were shaken by tremors or
their eyes blinked or
they came to work drugged or
drunk or both

it was terror and dismemberment
and the survivors
hunched on their stools wondering
who would be next

the supervisors brutalized us
and the supervisors
were in turn brutalized

by their superiors who
were in turn brutalized
by the Postmaster General
who always demanded
more for less
and the public brutalized
the Postmaster General
and it was finally
the little old lady
pruning her garden roses
who was the first cause
of misery for everybody:
Democracy at work

one night I asked,
"where's Hodges?"

(I don't know why but
I was always
the last to know anything
perhaps because I was white
and most of them were black)

there was no reply
about Hodges
who was the meanest soup
and *white*
to top it all

and I asked again
and somebody said
"he won't be around
for a while . . . "

and then
in pieces and bits
it was revealed to me:
Hodges had been knifed

164

in the parking lot
on the way to his car

and then
it was inferred
that everybody knew
who did it

"would it be anybody
I know?"
I smiled

it got very quiet
Big George put his mail down
stared at me
he stared at me a long time
then he turned
started sticking his letters again

and I said
"I wonder who's winning
the old ball game?"

"4 to 2,"
somebody said
"end of the 4th . . . "

Hodges never came back
and soon
I got out of there too.

the famous writer

▲▲▲

when I was a mailman
one of my routes was special:
a famous writer lived in one of those
houses,
I recognized his name on the letters,
he was a famous writer but not a very
good one,
and I never saw him
until this one morning when I was
hungover
I walked up to his house
and he was outside
he was standing in an old bathrobe,
he needed a shave and he looked ill
about 3 years from death
but he had this good looking woman
standing there with him
she was much younger than he
the sun shining through her full hair
and her thin dress,
I handed him his mail over the gate and
said, "I've read your books,"
but he didn't answer
he just looked down at the letters
and I said, "I'm a writer too . . . "
he still didn't answer,
he turned and walked off
and she looked at me
with a face that said nothing,
then turned and followed
him.

I moved on to the next house
where halfway across the lawn
a toy bulldog
came charging out
growling
with his putrid little eyes

seething
I caught him under the belly with
my left foot
and flung him up against a
picture window
and then I felt much better
but not
entirely
so.

darlings

▲▲

a world full of successful people's
sons
on bicycles
on the Hollywood Riviera
at 3:11 p.m.
on a Tuesday afternoon.

this is what some of the armies
died to save
this is what many of the ladies
desire:
these stuffed fractions
non-beings
pedaling along
or stopping to chat while
still seated upon their bikes
gentle breezes touching
undisturbed faces.

I understand very little of this
except maybe the armies killed the
wrong people
but they usually do:
they think the enemy are
those they are directed against
instead of those who
direct them:
the fathers of the
darlings.

goodbye

▲▲▲

goodbye Hemingway goodbye Celine (you died on the same day)
goodbye Saroyan goodbye good old Henry Miller goodbye Tennessee
Williams goodbye the dead dogs of the freeways goodbye all the
love that never worked goodbye Ezra it's always sad it's
always sad when people give and then are taken I accept I
accept and I will give you my automobile and my cigarette
lighter and my silver drinking chalice and the roof that kept
out most of the rain goodbye Hemingway goodbye Celine goodbye
Saroyan goodbye old Henry Miller goodbye Camus goodbye Gorky
goodbye the tightrope walker falling from the wire as the
blank faces look up then down then away
be angry at the sun, said Jeffers, goodbye Jeffers, I can only
think that the death of good people and bad are equally sad
goodbye D.H. Lawrence goodbye to the fox in my dreams and
to the telephone
it's been more difficult than I ever expected
goodbye Two Ton Tony goodbye Flying Circus
you did enough goodbye Tennessee you alcoholic speed-freak fag
I'm drinking an extra bottle of wine for you
tonight.

a strange moment
▲▲

as I was walking through this parking
lot
I saw a crowd gathered about two men
bloodied
in a fist fight
they were cursing and
they were breathing
heavily;
then one man caught a punch in the
mouth
crashed backwards into a
yellow Mercedes
bounced back
dug his fist into the other man's
gut.

I hated that crowd
they were watching like spectators at
a cockfight.
I pushed through
got between the men
caught a fist on the right
temple.

"all right," I said, "that's
enough, it's over."

they stood looking at each
other.

"that's it, go your
ways . . ."

one guy turned away but the other
guy charged,

"you son of a bitch!"

I caught him and held him
back . . .

"that's *it*, buddy, don't be
an asshole . . . "

for a moment it looked as if
he was going to swing on
me
then he put his hands
down and walked away through
the crowd.

I walked to my car
got in
started it
thinking, now what did
you do that for?
that was none of your
business

but I was smiling

I had altered a bit of
ugliness
into something
else
even though
such an act
was against
whatever vague
philosophy
I had
personal or
otherwise . . .

and pulling out of the
parking lot
and into traffic
it was crowded

171

and preparing to make a
lane change
I reached for the
blinker lever
touched the wrong
one
and my windshield wipers
began lashing
about
and then I
laughed: back to
normal: it sure felt
more
real.

beauti-ful

▲▲▲

one poet used to take
this stringy-haired blonde around
with him to poetry readings
and
she'd sit out in the audience
and now and then
just as he concluded a
poem
the blonde would
breathlessly say:
"beauti-ful . . . "

it made him look good
and I was a little jealous
of it
myself:
nobody had ever said that
about
one of my poems

and each time
after she said,
"beauti-ful . . . "
it made them
applaud.

he had her planted at
all his readings
this poet who was so good
with the ladies
he had a
gentle smile and
these artistic
dangling
hands
and he dangled
very well
elsewhere

173

it was
told.

I attended these readings
because I was living with a
sex-pot who *insisted* upon
going to them
and since our affair was
still fresh and
new
I made certain horrible
sacrifices

and *he* was reading
everywhere
in every little pitiful
hand-out
poetry hole in L.A.
and nearby
parts.

this one night
he had a new girl planted
in the audience
a tinted redhead
wearing fisherman's boots
and a cowboy hat
with a two-and-one-half foot
red feather
but she was as good as the
other:
at certain times
after certain poems
she too would utter the
word:
"beauti-full!"

and the applause would

follow ...

an hour later he was still
tirelessly going
on, and then he finished
one
and his new plant said it
again:
"beauti-ful ... "

and then it came
from the rear
from one of the back
seats:
*"No, it wasn't, it was a
piece of shit!"*

it was the stringy-blonde
standing up on
one of the seats
holding her paper cup
full of
Thunderbird

and then the applause came
it came and it
rose and it
rumbled
it was perfect and endearing
and unashamed

he had never heard applause
like
that ...

▲▲▲

and after that night

maybe a week later
I was alone
sitting up against the
headboard of the bed
the sex-pot was out
to a reading or
somewhere
and I was into another
beer
going through one of
those
throwaway tabloids
when I came across this
short notice
that a certain poet
had left for
New York City
to seek his fame and
fortune
there.

a beauti-ful city for a
beauti-ful guy, I thought,
bundling the tabloid
and dumping a 3 pointer into
the far-off
basket . . .

frozen food section

▲▲▲

he'd been fighting it for years:
that thing about
women in the supermarkets bending
over
or just
pushing their carts along—
he felt like grabbing a
buttock
and squeezing—
hardly a sexual
thing,
more like a weird joke,
just something else to do
besides the ordinary,
more in camaraderie than
desire;
he didn't know why his mind worked
that way
and he realized that
one of the niceties of
civilization
was the right to
unmolested privacy,
but there he was
rolling along
and he passed a lady
bending over in the
frozen food section
(she wasn't attractive:
her cheeks sagged beneath a
loose housedress)
and he saw his hand
go out—
there it goes, he
thought—
and the hand
grabbed
one of the buttocks

and squeezed,
then
let go . . .
it had felt like
an old beachball
underinflated
soft,
and he looked back
and smiled,
and the lady
screamed—
it was the scream
of one being murdered—
then after the tick of a
second
she stopped and yelled:
"That son of a bitch
assaulted me!"
(she pointed the deathly
finger attached to the end of her trembling
right arm at him)
"He grabbed my ass!"

he saw a fat man in a
yellow sweater and orange
walking shorts
running
toward him . . .
the fat man's face
was florid with
indignation.
the fat man circled
him
got an armlock on
him
from behind
jammed his shoulder up
into his neck

yelling,
"What's the matter
with you, buddy?"
the fat man had the most
terrible case of body
odor,
it was worse than the
pain in his
arm,
then out of nowhere
a cop arrived
and he heard the handcuffs
click
behind him
then felt the vicious
grip of the
cuffs
and a rap
behind his ear.

he was dragged through the
supermarket
and then outside.
it was early evening going into
night
and he was shoved into
the back seat of
the police car.

the faces of the crowd
looked in
at him
as the cop in front
spoke into the
radio
the red lights
whirled
and he remembered

the last thing
Meg had said:
"don't forget the
paprika, I *know*
you're going to
forget the
paprika . . ."

how do they get your number?

▲▲▲

the dogs of hell have claws like cats
and faces like women
and the doors of hell have numbers on
them
upside down
and to get through them
you have to walk with your hands
using your legs like giant
antennae:
in hell they give the answers
first
and ask the questions
later;
in hell you're always in love
with nothing to love,
and something hates you
for all the wrong reasons;
the cats of hell are all
bunghole
so dry
they want to wink but
can't
your father rules hell and your mother
licks his toes;
in this hell, it's never night
it's always morning
you're always getting up to the
sound of stinking alarms,
it's morning
more and more
leprous light like
the worst of your memories;
in this hell, there are no flames
just this moment
dangling intestines nailed to
mutilated palms
and the phone rings and

you pick it up
and somebody speaks through the
instrument
at 8:35 a.m.
"are you the poet,
Chinaski?
we all love you here and we
want you to read at our
bookstore...
all the beer you can drink, and
who knows? you old fuck, maybe
we can even find a piece of ass
for you somewhere! ha, ha, ha..."

182

the old gang

▲▲

of course, we were all fucked-up, I was suicidal but hitting the
shit out of the typer,
couldn't pick anything up off the floor: shirts, bottles, shorts,
towels, socks, cans,
I walked about naked and barefoot
stepping onto shards of glass
sometimes feeling it
sometimes not.
at times I tried to pick some of it
out
but I didn't want to get it all
because I'd read somewhere that the glass could work its way
through the bloodstream to the
heart and kill
you, yes . . .

there was a girl in and out,
a semi-girlfriend called K.
she came along mostly
but sometimes with a thin mad lady
called Sunflower,
and sometimes K. arrived with her
brother N.,
or sometimes all 3 arrived at
once.
anyhow, K. and N. and Sunflower were
all on drugs:
blacks, reds, yellows, whites,
coke.
I had a coke dealer who cut it so
fine
you got a headache just looking at
a line.
I was also on scotch, beer, wine
hitting the shit out of the typer
with K. and N. and Sunflower
banging on my door
usually at 4 or 5 a.m.

when I was up
anyhow.
they were more like sharks from hell
than friends
but K. had a fine body and very long red
hair
and she laid it on me
just often enough to keep me on her
leash.

meanwhile
I kept hitting the shit out of the typer
and some luck started
moneywise
which enabled me to escape that
neighborhood
and move to a small town down the
coast
where I continued to hit the shit out of
the typer,
even going back once to see K.
who was drying out in her mother's
home
and as she sat on the edge of her
bed
I told her,
"it's over between us, I don't know how
you got that grab on me . . . "

what a gang they had been,
driving their cars without pink
slips, license plates, driver's
licenses, just ripping and roaring, waiting
for the next drug
hit.

last I heard, they were clean,
Sunflower had
vanished,

but K. and her brother N.
surfaced in a recent issue of a national
magazine
sober
speaking as reliable sources
about my life
literary and
otherwise.
not that they were unkind, just
inaccurate.
it's well that they didn't
o.d.
but I hope it's their last
hurrah
regarding me,
and I'll never again quite
believe
what other people say
about
writers.

185

eulogy to a hell of a dame—

▲▲▲

some dogs who sleep at night
must dream of bones
and I remember your bones
in flesh
and best
in that dark green dress
and those high-heeled bright
black shoes,
you always cursed when you
drank,
your hair coming down you
wanted to explode out of
what was holding you:
rotten memories of a
rotten
past, and
you finally got
out
by dying,
leaving me with the
rotten
present;
you've been dead
28 years
yet I remember you
better than any of
the rest;
you were the only one
who understood
the futility of the
arrangement of
life;
all the others were only
displeased with
trivial segments,
carped
nonsensically about

nonsense;
Jane, you were
killed by
knowing too much.
here's a drink
to your bones
that
this dog
still
dreams about.

sky sign

▲▲▲

the falcons have come to the city
and are swooping down
carrying off the pigeons.
the dogs and cats
look back and
run for cover
as a moving shadow falls
between them
and the sun.

I too am worried
stand beneath a palm leaf
and light a cigarette.

I watch the falcon glide
gracefully
above the telephone wires,
it is a beautiful
thing
that falcon
from this distance,
and, of course,
it makes me think
of death
and death is perfectly
proper
yet I throw my cigarette
down
stamp it out,
look up at the bird:
"you son-of-a-bitch . . . "

I turn
walk through the doorway
and into the house
as the telephone
rings.

a valentine gift

▲▲

I sit looking dumbly at this stuffed red devil on my desk. I am in
a fix. it
gets like this
sometimes: the magic is elsewhere.

it was with old man Shoemaker at the races
today: he rode the first four winners:
3/5, 2 to one, 6 to one, 8 to one.

you know, sometimes I run out of the money all
night: the poems rear up in the gate, break
their legs, run the wrong way, never finish

but it's the fault of the jock: he's got his
ass on backwards, his mind is up in the palm
trees.

maybe my problem is that I had 5 winners at
the track today. maybe that's all I think
I need.

I knew a guy once who wrote and he too
often went to the track. he always had
the same story for me: "I went bust! I
even blew the bus money home! Jesus Christ,
I had to walk *five* miles!"

then he'd get to his room and write and
he'd go bust
all over again.

well, I think the idea of the track or the
roulette wheel or whatever else is around is
so that we don't have to sit around all day
thinking, I am a writer.

and the idea of sitting down to the typer
is the same, you don't want to sit there

thinking, I am a writer . . .

the stuffed red devil looks at me and it
looks like me: fat nose, slit eyes, surly
grin

as some guy on the radio plays bad piano
music all over us
the son of a bitch looks drunk as
his forked tail rests upon a
piece of
blank typing paper.

a sweaty day in August

▲▲

we were starving
yet drinking
living in a cheap
apartment
always behind
in the rent
there wasn't
much else to
do
but screw

and I was
working away
pumping
pumping
determined to
make it

I had failed
at
everything
else

I wanted to
make it
at *that*

I groaned
pumped
flailed

5 minutes
ten minutes

so near
so near

it was so

ridiculous
in a certain
sense

and
finally
I felt myself
nearing a
climax

victory
at last

and
at the exact moment
I climaxed

for no reason
the alarm clock
went off

and I rolled
off of her
laughing and
spurting

and she asked
angrily, "what's
the matter
with you?"

and that made
it
worse

I kept laughing
and she ran
to the bathroom

slammed the
door

and I
wiped off
on the sheet

as the clock
sat there
innocently
reading:
2:30 p.m.

macho man

▲▲▲

the phone rings.
I answer.
it's a woman.
she says,
"you are a sick
fucker and I thought
I'd tell you
that . . . "

she hangs up.

I am supposedly
unlisted.

it rings
again.

"you wrote this
macho bullshit
but you're
probably a
fag, you
probably want to
suck
black dick!"

she hangs
up.

I am watching
the Johnny Carson
Show.
he amuses
me,
he's so
straight-backed
dressed in his
high school

194

go-to-dance
suit.
he touches
his nose
his necktie
the back of
his neck.
he's a dead
giveaway:
he wants
desperately
to be all right
just like his
audience.

it rings again.

"you don't know
what a *real*
woman is!
if you ever met
a *real* woman
you wouldn't know
what to do
with her!"

she hangs
up.

Carson jokes about
his jokes being
so bad
but he has probably
consumed and
murdered
more writers than
Bobby Hope.

195

then *she's*
back:
"why do you keep listening to
me?
why don't you
hang up?"

I hang up
then take
the phone
off the
hook.

Carson has
finished his
monologue.
smiles.
is delicately
concerned
yet
pleased.
he goes into
his little golf
swing
as the commercial
descends
upon
me.

it's just another
dull night
in San Pedro
as all my
male servants
Kitcha Kubee
Des Man DeAblo
La Tabala
and

196

Swine Herd Sam
stand
with their
black dicks
extended.

I decide to have
my unlisted
number
changed
but meanwhile
remote control
the tv
off,
wave the
fellows
away
and reach for
the pages of
Sam Beckett
as my
cross-eyed white
cat
leaps upon the
bedcovers.

**note upon the love letters
of Beethoven:**

▲▲

think: if Ludwig were alive today
tooling along in his red sports
car
roof down
he'd pick up all these mad
hard cases on the boulevards
we'd get music like we
never heard before
and he'd still never
ever find his
Beloved.

how I got started

▲▲

it has taken me decades to realize
why I was usually chosen over the
6 or 7 candidates for those
paltry shipping clerk jobs
in those small business houses
across the nation.
first, I was big—
which meant I could lift heavy
objects.
second, I was ugly—
which meant I was no threat to
the secretaries.
third, I looked dumb—
which meant I was too stupid
to steal.

if I had been running a business
and a guy like me had come to apply
for a job
I would have hired him
right away.

which is rather
the way I ended up anyhow
in another kind of
business.

Krutz

▲▲▲

I was in Mannheim when my agent phoned me
at the hotel, he said Krutz wanted to have
dinner with the whole gang, and I told
my agent, o.k.
I thought that was very nice of Krutz
because it was a large gang—my agent, my
girlfriend, a French movie producer and his
girlfriend, and also
3 or 4 other people who were hanging on,
maybe more than 3 or 4.

the next evening found us at the most
expensive restaurant in town, at a large
reserved table with a head waiter and 2 or
3 additional waiters.

Krutz had his girlfriend with him and we
had drinks and appetizers, then some-
body remarked how young Krutz was to be
a leading publisher in Germany.
Krutz just smiled around his
cigar.

Krutz published me.
I smiled around my
cigarette.

my agent was there with his wife; I don't
know how many were at the table, perhaps
12, and I thought what a good guy
Krutz was, not only for publishing me
but also for wining and dining all these
people.

everybody ordered, drank, and waited;
the food was slow to arrive and the
bottles of wine emptied and more arrived via
those gently smiling waiters, and we

all laughed and talked and smoked and
drank,
and then the food arrived—such magic:
frogs legs, crab legs, steaks so tender you
could cut them with your fork; and lobsters,
all manner of strange foodstuffs—onions,
greens, creams and gravies, olives, pickles,
delightful unknown specialties;
and hot bread so soft the butter ran through;
it was royal food, food beyond our ken,
and we ate and drank, and finally finished,
and then we drank some more,
they ran out of our favorite
wine and we ordered a new one, and then
it began to get late, quite late, and the waiters
were slower and slower bringing the bottles and
they were no longer smiling, and soon we stopped
laughing and just talked, and then the
bottles stopped arriving;
the head waiter walked up and placed the
bill in the center of the table on a large silver
platter
and it just sat there
as the waiters stood and waited as
we waited.

the bill was near Krutz and we all watched
Krutz but he didn't reach
except into his coat where he ex-
tracted a large and expensive cigar . . .
he took the cigar and leisurely began licking
it, turning and licking it, then
he came with the lighter, stuck the cigar
into his mouth, lit it, inhaled contentedly,
exhaling a slow and beautiful stream of gentle blue
aromatic smoke . . .

then he waited.

the message was obvious
to almost everybody.

I looked at my agent, but he was immune to the
tragedy, he was smiling and talking to
somebody.

I didn't have the money
and I looked around the table:
it was an unbelievable scene as my girlfriend poked
her elbow into my side whispering, "what the hell's
going on?"

Krutz leaned further back in his chair, sucked,
blew out another langorous stream of blue smoke.
then, suddenly, the waiters came forward, removed
all the plates, all the bottles, and all that was
left were our empty wine glasses and our ashtrays.
we all sat there and the waiters waited and the
head waiter waited and there was no more laughing,
no more talking (well, my agent was still busy
talking and smiling away at somebody).
it was agony, it was dirty dirty agony while
Krutz smoked . . .

finally, the French director saved us all, he waved
his credit card and the head waiter moved in for the
kill . . .

▲▲▲

we were able to leave then and we met later
outside near the automobiles where Krutz lit a fresh
cigar and his girlfriend gave me a bag of apples
from their garden
which I
thanked them for . . .

▲▲▲

back at the hotel
my girlfriend and I each
ate an apple
and she said,
"these are great apples, these German apples..."
and I said,
"yes, they are."

and when she went to the bathroom
I took my drink and the bag of apples and
I went out on the balcony...
we were on the top floor
and I hurled the apples
one by one
into the night
into the street
and toward the park
and grabbing the last apple
I really zoomed it
almost going over the side
myself
but, of course, I didn't
and I turned and walked back
in there
feeling better
but not
much.

not to worry

▲▲▲

he sits there
big in his chair
contented
and he tells me he
walked out on a
wife and two kids
changed his name
started all over
again.

his new woman
brings us
fresh bottles of
beer.

she's pregnant.
they've already
named the
baby:

Nero.

dear pa and ma

▲▲

my father liked Edgar Allan
Poe
and my mother liked *The
Saturday Evening Post*
and she died first
the priest waving smoking
incense above her
casket
and my father followed
a year or so later
and in that purple velvet coffin
his face looked like ice
painted yellow

my father never liked
what I wrote: "people
don't want to read this
sort of thing."

"yes, Henry, " said my
mother, "people like to
read things that make
them happy."

they were my earliest
literary critics
and
they both were
right.

not all that bad

▲▲▲

was sitting here, drinking a glass of
wine
the phone rang, I left the drink
to answer in the other
room.
came back in a few minutes
sat down
picked up the glass
felt something moving in my
mouth,
Jesus Christ!
I spit it out into the
ashtray:
a fly
wiggling there . . .
I picked up the wine glass,
walked into the bathroom
dumped the contents,
then the glass slipped out of
my hand
and rattled in the wash basin.
I rinsed out my mouth, the glass,
then walked back in
poured a new drink.
the fly was still wiggling . . .
there we were,
a wino fly and a wino man
at 1:30 a.m.
and now there's another fly
whirling and buzzing
above me
no doubt wanting to join
the party.
well, it could be worse:
I could be drinking with
things that can't
fly
either with their bodies

206

or any other
way.
and you can't
spit *them*
out.

dogs

▲▲

someplace in Arizona
at the dog
races.

the dogs were
great
and the boys
led them out
on the track
junior highschool boys
in orange jackets
who should have been home
studying
contemporary history or
biology.

the night was
calm
the track looped in front
of those jagged
mountains
that stood above those
lizard-and-snake-crawled
sands,
the track was my
El Dorado and the crowd was
small
and I came up with
75% winners
none the actual
betting
favorite.

and as she drove me back
she was silent.
she knew I hadn't been thinking
of her
although I had once loved her

very much, and I felt sad
for *her*,
she was very straight at the
wheel
her hair falling into her
face,
she said, "now I guess you want
to get drunk?"

"of course,"
I said.

she was always pissed and that
pissed her more and she hit the throttle
and the speedometer on her dash only went to
85
and the needle went past that
and my window was open and the
air rushed in
and the mountains sped by
and cars leaped aside as she
approached
but a jack rabbit didn't make
it—
one the dogs had failed
to catch—
and the dead carcass was
thrown against the
windshield,
there was a splash of
blood and then the carcass was
gone, and I thought, fuck it, death
I accept
you.

but it didn't happen, we
skidded to a stop
in front of her court

and we got out
and went inside
where her sister was
waiting,
and we sat there for
several hours
talking
laughing
drinking tea
(for them)
wine for
me
talking and
laughing
as if everything was
all right
instead of mutilated
and murdered
forever.

hey, Ezra, listen to this

▲▲

I think I learned much about writing when
I read those issues of *The Kenyon Review*
over 40 years ago
the light of the starving library room
falling across my starving hands
holding fat pages full of
deliberate glorious
rancor

those critics

those spoiled fat gnats
bellicose

very fine energy
more fulfilling than my
park bench

I learned that words could
beat the hell out of
anything

they were
better than paint
better than music
better than clay
stone
or their
counterparts

yet
wasn't it strange
that all I wanted to do then was
lift the skirt of the librarian and
look at her legs and
grab her panties?

I didn't do it.

literary fame can be the consequence
of knowing
when to go wild
and how.

truce

▲▲▲

I need to walk down a sidewalk
somewhere
on a shady afternoon
find a table
outside a cafe
sit down
order a drink
and I want to sit there
with that drink
and I want
a fly to land
on that table.
then
in the background
I want to hear somebody
laugh.
then
I want to see
a woman walk by
in a green dress.
I want to see
a dog walk by
a fat dog
with short brown hair and
with grinning eyes.
I want to die
sitting there.
I want to die
upright
my eyes still
open.
I want an airplane
to fly overhead.
I want a woman
to walk by
in a blue dress.
then I want
that same fat dog

with short brown hair and
grinning eyes
to come walking by
again.
that will be
enough
after all the
other
after everything
else.

the gentleman and the bastard

▲▲▲

the L.A. Rams in those days had
what some call color—
each game seemed to go down to
the last second
always before crowds of
100,000 in the good times of
the fifties.

it seemed that the team
who had the ball
last
won the game.

the Rams had two great
ends: Tom Fears and
Crazy Legs Hirsch
and two
huge grinding fullbacks:
Tank Younger and
Deacon Dan Towler

and two
quarterbacks:
Bob Waterfield and
Norm Van Brocklin.

Waterfield
being from U.C.L.A.
was the starter
got the good
press

he was
talented and a
gentleman

but his
back-up

215

Dutch
Van Brocklin
was a nasty
backwoods s.o.b.
without a good word
for
anybody

but after Waterfield
got the team
in the
hole

here would come
Dutch
halfway through the
third quarter
or more often
at the beginning
of the
fourth

fresh and
mean

points
behind
going for broke
throwing
for broke

those high
towering
passes, perfectly
leading his
swift ends
time after
time

always fighting
the clock

and then
with the other team
dropping back
for the
pass

here would come
Younger or
Towler
straight up the
middle
breaking through
tacklers as if
they were cotton-
wood
branches.

Dutch pulled out
many a game
and if he didn't
win it
he came so
close
you could cry
with fury
at that last
perfect pass
dropped as the
gun
went off.

Waterfield vs.
Van Brocklin
they called it The
Great Quarterback

Debate.

the press sided
with Waterfield
but the facts and
the drama sided
with
Dutch

always working
against the
clock
cursing his
linemen in the
huddle
for missed
blocks
cursing his
ends for not
getting down-
field fast
enough

he was the
guy from
out of
town
trying to
clean up the
mess

he wanted to
get it
done
somehow

no matter
what the

hell

and he
usually
did.

early this
year
long before his
time
Waterfield
died

and still
playing
backup
Dutch died
90 days
later.

Waterfield was
a very fine
player
but there was never
any Great Quarterback
Debate
for me.

my heart went
out
to Dutch

and I haven't
been
to any Ram
games
since.

bad action

▲▲

I got a seat down front and started
working on my figures
and a man in a red shirt and red
pants
sat down two seats away
opened a brown paper bag
and began chewing on a sandwich and
potato chips.
I got up, moved several seats
away,
then I heard a man's voice behind
me:
"let's see, there are seven of us,
aren't there?"
and there were: women and men and
children.

I walked downstairs to the crapper,
found a booth, closed the door,
sat down and began working on my
figures again.

there was a rap from the stall to
my left:
"hey buddy . . . hey, buddy!"

"yeah?" I answered.

"get down on your knees, slip your
cock under the partition and I'll
give you the best blow job you
ever had!"

I got out of there fast, went back
upstairs, found a seat, sat down
and then I felt something under my
right foot: a dead wren.
another reminder of death.

the public address system
came on:
"Ladies and Gentlemen, the Flag of
the United States of America!"

we all stood up.
the flag went up.
we all sat down.

sometimes being at the racetrack
is worse than being in the
county jail.

fall out

▲▲

they are closing the auto plants
out here in California
but a major company is promising
employment to laid-off workers
who will transfer to an Oklahoma
plant
travel expenses
paid.

so now
many of the families are
making the trek
in long caravans of cars
full of children and
possessions

just as in the 30's
their elders had come here
from Oklahoma
in the same way

now they're going back
to Oklahoma
with California accents

Grandchildren of the
Dust Bowl

because Japanese cars are
smaller, cheaper,
better

it's like a little bit of
Hiroshima
in return

or a Japanese horror
movie

with an all-American
cast.

my friend

▲▲▲

I loved bar room fights.
I fought the biggest meanest men
I could find.
the patrons thought I was
brave.

but it was something else, something
that walked and slept and sat with
me. it ate with me when I ate,
it drank with me when I drank.
I saw it everywhere: in loaves
of bread, on the back of a mouse
running up the wall, I saw it through
torn window shades, I saw it
in the bodies of beautiful women;
I never saw it in the sun but I saw it
in the rain and I noted it in in-
sects; and I saw it riding in buses
and trolley cars;
I saw it in the dresser drawer when I
pulled it open,
I saw it in the faces of
bosses with their dumb wet lips and
little rivet eyes: blue, brown,
green;
I heard it in the click of timeclocks,
saw it spread like powder across the
faces of my landladies;
I saw it on bar
stairways
leading to the 2nd
floor of some rooming house in
Houston, in New Orleans, in St. Louis,
in L.A., in Frisco;
and I saw it in the doorknobs and I saw
it in the rooms, sitting on the
beds
waiting nicely . . .

and in some bar
after hours of drinking
somebody says, "hey, Hank, you
ever tried Big Eddie?"
Big Eddie grins, I see it in his
teeth, I finish my beer,
nod at him, get up, walk to
the rear entrance, Big Eddie and
the crowd following, and outside
I see it in the moon and the
bricks
as the patrons lay their bets
I am the underdog, and as Big
Eddie charges I see it in his
feet and on the buttons of
his shirt and I hear a horn
sound somewhere far off, and
it's as decent a thing as a man
can know.

a patriot of life

▲▲

the old guy
next door
he's
83

old Charlie

he runs the
American flag
from the roof
of his
garage

his wife
screams and
nags at
him

so
he has
his own
little place

a shack
he built
next to
the garage

CAPTAIN'S
QUARTERS
he has
painted
across the
door . . .

I go over
to see
old Charlie

I'm in
trouble of
sorts
and I
find him
in his
CAPTAIN'S
QUARTERS

he's nearly
totally
deaf

I have to
scream
so he can
hear:

"*Hey, you got
a crowbar
I can
use?*"

"try
my wife,"
he says.

I yell
again:

"*I need a
crowbar!*"

"oh," he
smiles,
"I thought
you said
'a crow'."

I thank
him
tell him
that's not
what
I want

and leave
him
there
sorting
among the
thumbscrews
and
the
ten penny
nails

some
guy
old Charlie

oblivious to
solutions

yet

alone
like the
mountain over
the sea

he makes
a little
of the darkness
retreat.

girls

▲▲▲

I used to spend 3 days a week
driving one or the other of the
girls to various pharmacies
on Hollywood Boulevard.

how they got their prescriptions
I don't know
whether they fucked their
doctors or murdered somebody
I don't know

but they got them.
it was some circus.

one of the girls
phoned me: "Eddie is trying
to get my prescription! tell
Eddie to leave me alone!"

I got Eddie on the phone and
told him that I was going to
kick his ass, that I was on my
way over to do just that.

Eddie was her brother.
he lived there.

when I got there
he was gone.

"he couldn't find the pre-
scription," she told me, "I
had it in my mouth. I almost
swallowed it . . . "

she showed me the wadded wet piece of
paper, unfolded it and said,
"let's go . . . "

I don't know what it meant to
me.
usually it meant that when we got
back to my place and I took
some pills with the booze
I'd do something stupid
like busting out the
bathroom mirror or
slicing up my coffee table
with my buck knife.
although the girls looked
fairly good
there was not much sex
involved

it meant
letting one or the other of them
out of my car
at the prescription department
of some cheap pharmacy on
Hollywood Boulevard
at 10:35 a.m.
then looking for parking
finding one of them later
wobbling on high heels
looking helpless
but really totally vicious
snarling off any stupid dreamers
in the sidewalk mob

then seeing me,
moving forward
to another day and night
of pills and
alcohol
uppers downers
vodka wine beer brandy
it didn't matter

until we were petrified
out of existence

until the next
time.

ass but no class
▲▲

one time
there was Rene who
had me drive her to a
department store
just before Xmas
and we walked around
as she stocked her
shopping cart with
little goodies, then
she said, "listen, I
can't pay for these
things, can you buy
them for me?"
"nothin' doin',"
I told her.
"listen," she said,
"you buy this stuff
and I'll fuck you
like you never been
fucked before."
so, I paid.
it came to
$145.63

at the counter she
happened to meet
her friends,
Jeff and Clara
and they
talked.

"listen," she finally
told them, "why don't
we all go to Hank's and
have a drink?"

we went.
we sat around with the

drinks.
we drank those and had
some more.
Jeff and Clara
didn't leave.
I saw Rene lean over
to Clara one time and
whisper something to
her.

I got it.
she was saying, don't
leave me here alone with
him.

they all sat about
and then Clara and Jeff
said they had to leave
and Rene said she had to
leave too.

I left it
like that.
I let Rene leave.

she took her purchases
with her.

she was a young girl
and I was an old
man.

I watched them
walking away together
up the walk,
Rene with her
victorious
swish.

we'd been to bed
2 or 3
times

she thought, now,
it was enough for me
if she came around
once in a while
wired on speed
while we played
Scrabble all
night.

as they walked away,
I thought,
what an *unimaginative*
whore,
she has just walked away
from a potential
$200,000.00

I walked into the kitchen
pulled out a beer,
had a hit
and relegated her to a
lifetime of poverty
worse than the one
that I was living
at the
moment.

overhead mirrors
▲▲

I wouldn't say it was a particularly low time, it was
a time and I tried to adjust spiritually
to most matters.
which meant: not expecting much and not getting much.

but sickness is another matter.
I was living in a cheap court in Hollywood
in between women
and I was buying coke, really
low-grade crap, sniffing that with
beer and scotch.
I got mentally very depressed and physically
sick.
I couldn't eat.
it got so I just ingested
coke, scotch and beer.

one morning it really got to me, I was trembling,
having visions . . .
I couldn't even drink water . . .
I was
dying.

the only friends I had were a nudey dancer and
a guy who operated a porno bookstore. they
came by.

"listen, this is it," I told them, "I'm
dying . . . "

"we'll fix you up," said the porno bookstore
guy (who was also selling me
the watered-down coke).
the nudey dancer shacked with him.

he came back with something pink in a
bottle.
"take this," he said.

that was about noon.

about 6 p.m. the phone rang.
I picked it up.

"yes?"

it was the porno guy.
"Hank?"

"yes . . . "

"listen, Babs and I aren't working tonight,
we're going to a motel with over-
head mirrors and X-rated tv, we're going to
relax and fuck."

"good luck . . . "

"I know you're sick, so we're going to
give you the phone number at the
motel so you can call us in case of
trouble . . . "

"sure . . . "

"got a pencil?"

"yeh . . . "

"it's . . . "

he gave me the number.
I didn't have a pencil, I couldn't
move.

"thanks," I said.

▲▲▲

it was one of those nights you remember.
(if you don't fight death it will
just move in.)
at times I
got up
and walked around
turned the radio off and on, flushed the toilet
now and then, ran all the faucets in the place,
then shut them off, turned the lights off and
on, got back on the bed, rested but not too long,
got up, sipped water out of the tap,
sat in a chair and took some coins
out of my pocket and counted them: 25, 26, 27
cents . . .
I kept turning the water off and on, the lights
off and on, counting the coins and also very
sensibly putting one shoe parallel to the
other shoe and so forth . . .
as I went about my business I noticed that the
clock hardly moved:
the time always the same: 3:21 a.m.
then all at once, within a
minute
I noticed light coming in under the blinds—
daylight arriving
and when I saw that
I felt a bit better
went to bed
and slept flat on my belly as
usual . . .

the next night I was sitting on my couch
drinking a beer and eating a fried egg
sandwich between 2 slices of very dry
bread

when

my friends
the nudey dancer and the porno guy
came in.

"how you feeling?" he asked.

"o.k., except it's my last beer and
I'm broke."

"shit, man, come on down to our place,
we got plenty of everything . . ."

they did.
lovely place. I stayed with the beer
except for two vodka sevens and one little
yellow pill
and they had the stereo on
but not too loud
and I stayed
smoked two bombers
drank 18 or 19 beers
thanked them and walked back
home . . .

the next morning I didn't puke.
I got up, took a good crap, took a
lukewarm bath, dressed and walked to the
corner of
Hollywood and Western
put a dime in the box
got a *Herald-Examiner*,
remembering decades back when there
was a newspaper in L.A.
called the *Herald-Express* and another
called the *Examiner*
and they merged rather than

kill each other off,
and carrying that paper back
I felt that I had lived a long
time
though not a very wonderful one,
I took the paper back to my place,
sat on the couch
and began to read it
fascinated, finally, with what the
other people
were doing.

girls from nowhere

▲▲▲

the girls from nowhere came
and sat in my chairs and
drank and smoked with me
and got into my bed
like toy children
unreal

but
at times
there were
tiny bits of
marvelous magic

but most of
the time
they were
unattached
to everything

the sky
the ground
the sea
the voice
the laughter
or
the luck.

they were just
going on.

they had some
courage
but not much
kindness.

I always felt
better when
they left

and was
unsure why
they
returned

always with
some story of
being abused
which was
probably
true.

but
they were
sometimes tiring
during the long
nights
with their
cursing and their
embittered
slurred
speeches
much hair
falling into
those faces.

the girls from
nowhere
had much
to say.

at times
I found this
(and them)
interesting
enough

explaining it

all
with
verve

kicking
their
long legs with
spiked
heels

yet
they always brought
trouble
one way or the
other

especially if I
began to
care
too much.

then
they knew
what to
do

and they
did
it.

making it

▲▲

I was a frenetic wretch of a man
I was with R. and C. and M. and L. and
we were always fucking and there were arguments
there was unhappiness and my penis hurt
from constant ejaculation
I was sucking breasts
I was down between thighs
I was on top
I was on the bottom
I couldn't remember the last 7 times.

I'd get spasms just sitting in a chair
drinking a beer.
I sat on my reading glasses.
my veins were knotted in large bunches at my temples.
I got toothaches
backaches
headaches
I got flat tires everywhere
I got constipated
I didn't comb my hair
but I was fucking—
sometimes I'd be down there
and she'd be down there
"now when I do it," she'd say,
"you do it . . ."

I was standing in bathrooms with wet
washrags
continually.
I couldn't clean the ring out of my toilet
but I was fucking and fighting
with R. and C. and M. and L.
they were always threatening to leave me
and I just couldn't understand them.

I wasn't good at war with women
I was too serious and they were

243

too good at it.
they were smarter than I was
and I felt worse and worse.
the more I fucked them and fought
with them
the worse I felt.

I became totally inept:
I couldn't answer the doorbell or the
telephone,
I failed to make the bed
I couldn't shave
I couldn't brush my teeth
I got WARNING notices from the
phone company
from the water and power people
from the IRS
from Franchise Tax Board
I did send off for my license plate tab
but when it arrived
I promptly lost it . . .

but I was fucking
I got some groans from
R. and C. and M. and L. that sounded
real
but I never did ask any of them if
they climaxed.
I sure as hell did.
continually.
the skin of my penis
was raw to the touch—like fire—
the m.d. said no v.d.
he said, "Christ, give that thing a
rest. take a year off. find some
other hobby."

but I continued.

I laughed but without happiness.
I had ulcer attacks.
I aged five years in six months.
yet my jealousies
consumed me, my imagination whirled
counter-clockwise in my brain.
I drove my auto recklessly
I lost jobs, found jobs, lost jobs,
drank and smoked continually.
I had insomnia
the skin peeled off the
backs of my hands.
I had no appetite but I kept fucking and
I didn't know how to get out
of it.
I was caught there,
between legs lifted ceiling-
ward,
a man
doing it
again and again and again—
bedsheets, bedsteads, shades, curtains,
pillows, tits, breasts, buttocks.
the smell of love sometimes and the smell of sex
always
with R. and C. and M. and L. . . .

but oftentimes
at the most intense and passionate
moments
I wished that I could be that
lonely fellow again
sitting in a movie house with
my bag of popcorn
as all about me
couples sat
side by side
together.

naked at 92 degrees

▲▲

little to do on a HOT night but swat at
small BUGS and consider the
STOCKPILES

even SEX now brings the threat of DEATH
through new and incurable
DISEASES

now YOU must be prepared to
DIE for your
LOVE

and now
it seems
more and more
we are just sitting
WAITING for
NOTHING

now you must be
prepared to DIE
for
NOTHING

the jails and madhouses
are
FULL
yet there's no
PANIC

not even
here

I kill a flying
insect as the Tower of
Pisa
leans MORE and
MORE.

on this HOT
night
in this HOT
room
sucking on
CIGARETTES
and
too LAZY to
PISS
too late to
CARE
we lack the
IMAGINATION to
even
SCREAM.

now
▲▲▲

well,
now some eat to forget and some drink to forget and some
make love to forget
and some take drugs to forget and some go to movies to
forget
and some sleep to forget and some travel to forget and
some work crossword puzzles to forget and some
chop wood to forget and some
stand on their heads to forget
but what do they do to remember?
you can't tell me many things they do to remember
like I write this poem to remember to forget

some go to the circus to forget
and some fly gliders to forget
some mix salads
some pole vault
some shave their skulls
some walk through fire
as the water boils over
as the president laces his shoes
as the can can girls can can
there are whole oceans full of the tears of agony
and my father sits across the room from me now with
his big fat jowls of shimmering slime
knowing I'm typing about him now
knowing that I've failed to remember to forget
I switch on the radio
get Stravinsky
note the dirt under my
fingernails

he's
the best.

nice try

▲▲▲

best dream I ever
had
I could
fly
in this
dream

I flew over
fields and the
dry brown
hills
and
below me
men, women and
children
were
running

and then
my flying
mechanism began to
fail
falter
and I began to
fall
slowly toward
them
and they
reached up their
hands
and tried to
grab me
but through sheer
and
damnable will
I forced myself to
fly
up

again
out of their
reach

and with that
it got
easier and
easier
and I flew
up
up
through the clouds
and out into
the
sunlight.

when I awakened
I was on the
drunktank floor
of the old
Lincoln Heights jail
at North Avenue
21
and not only
didn't I have any
wings
all I had was
my property slip
and somebody was
puking
into the
toilet.

maybe I'd be
an angel
some other
time.

the puzzle

▲▲

my neighbor is a nice guy but he utterly
confounds me:
he gets up very early in the morning, goes
to work;
his wife works, they have two lovely
children;
he is home in the evening, I sometimes see
the children, briefly see the
wife;
by 9 p.m. all the lights in their house are
out;
and his days repeat themselves like this;
he seems a fairly intelligent man
in his early 30's;
the only explanation for his
routine is that he must
enjoy his
work
believe in
God,
sex,
family.

I don't know why
but over there
I always expect some windows to break suddenly
I expect to hear some screams
hear obscene language
see lights at 3 a.m.
see
flying bottles

but for 5 years now
his routine has remained the
same

so
I take care of these other

things for
him
which
I don't think his wife
appreciates:
"Hank, I could have
called the cops
many times but
I haven't."

sometimes
I'd like to call the
cops on *them*
but I don't think the cops
would understand my
complaint

their red lights flashing,
white-faced in
dark blue:

"Sir, there's no
law
against what they
are
doing . . ."

Big John of Echo Park

▲▲

his wife worked and bought his
pills
and he sat in the big chair
six-feet-two and two-hundred-and
forty-five pounds
with
two thousand pounds of useless
junk spread
about the house.
he gathered and added to
this crap
almost every night
when he was
high.
scavenging the backyards and
garbage cans of the
neighborhood

and I
sat with him often
and we took pills
in mid-afternoon as
the world cranked
away.

he
was really a brilliant
fellow:
one day I
helped him carry out
2 weeks of dirty
dishes
and we spread them
about
in the yard
and he washed them down with
the garden
hose.

we took the
pills and
we talked for
hours
days
and he recorded it
all on tape, most of
it useless
gibberish, most of
it
mine.

I saw him
the other day
and he looked as fine
as ever,
hadn't worked in
30 years
not even
at his writing:
the same
22 pages of very
strong
maybe great
writing
re-appearing
in the magazines
and given
from memory
at his
readings.

he knows that
ambition is
bullshit
shuck
and he can
point to

the fact
that
over the
decades
it has
destroyed
all those
we once
knew.

"you still with
Sally?" I asked, about
his wife.

"shit," he
answered, "do you
think I'd *ever* let
a good thing like
that
get away?"

he always had this
way of
easily mastering
any
conversation.

it's a
good thing
for many of us
in this stinking
racket
that he just
doesn't like to
type
too much.

on being recognized

▲▲

the young girl found me at the track,
told me how much she liked my poems, stories,
novels.

when such moments occur
(and they do, at times)
I find it difficult to respond
because one does not walk about thinking,
I am a writer.
in fact, when you're not writing
you're not a writer.
one forgets.
and so,
one is never quite ready when
reminded.

so there she was, "glad you like my stuff,"
I responded without any originality, then
I became worldly and added, "when you see
my books be sure to buy them . . . "

"oh sure, sure," she said
her beautiful eyes very close, her body
very close.

"I gotta bet now," I told
her.

"yes, of course," she
answered.

I walked off thinking about how possibly
thousands of young girls might be reading my books
in their beds.

then as I walked along
I happened to look down
I had been in a hurry to make the first

race: I had on one black shoe and one
brown shoe.

original at last, I thought, hope it lasts
until the next time I see a
typewriter.

I made my bet and then went downstairs where
the young girl wouldn't see
the black shoe and the brown shoe
on the famous
writer.

love

▲▲▲

answering a letter to somebody in Alaska
the radio has been tuned in to a new wave
group and I have listened to their work
and found that the favorite word in
all their songs is
"love."

the person in Alaska is young but dying,
considering suicide, and he wants to know
what I think
about it all, he wants an answer, he needs
one
and it's a difficult letter to write
as the young boy on the radio sings
"walk out on me now, baby, and I'm
done..."

I change the station, get some classical
music, then my phone rings, it rings and
it rings
on a hot July night

nothing ever goes as it should, it
goes as it must, and I move toward the
telephone
even as warheads are
constantly shuttled
underground
on hidden railroad tracks
so that
enemy missiles cannot
locate them

I pick up the phone, say "hello,"
and
wait.

the hustle
▲▲

the readings in those college towns were hell,
of course, but I liked the flying in and out,
drinking on the planes, and I liked the hotels,
the impersonal rooms.

the nights before the readings were best,
stretched out on the bed in a strange town,
the fifth of whiskey on the night stand,
and, you know, those hotels were *quiet* . . .
those southern hotels
and especially those midwestern hotels.

it was a stupid hustle but it beat the factories,
I knew that, but it was humorous to me
and ridiculous that
I was accepted as a POET
but after I examined the work of my compatriots
I no longer minded taking the money
and after hearing some of them read
I hardly felt the impostor at all
although I knew I was a bit crazy
especially after drinking
and that
I just might
some night
take out my hose and start pissing from the
podium . . .

some of the profs must have guessed
for after I accepted an invitation to read
most wrote back to me:
"I hope you won't cost me my job . . . "

second best, I remember
the adoring eyes of the coeds
but first of all, like I said, I liked
all those hotel rooms the nights before the
readings

me sitting up in bed, smoking, sucking
on the fifth, sick of looking at the poems,
thinking, if I can fool them it's all right,
worse have, many more will . . .
no wonder this world isn't very
much

then I'd go for a big gulp from the fifth,
say, at 2:30 a.m.—
it was just like being back
home.

sex and / or love
▲▲

in my dreams
I can hit a home run almost
every time up
if I want
to.
I *could* bat
.980

but soon they'd
just walk me
every time
I got to the
plate.

so,
that's what
I tell my
women:
I've got to
strike out
now and then
just to make it
interesting . . .

don't over-do
it, they
say.

I've got to keep
a low profile,
I tell them,
or I'll get eaten
up.

that's when the
screaming starts

you know, the way

they talk you'd
think I wasn't
trying
at
all.

funny

▲▲▲

sometimes you are liked for all the wrong
reasons
or hated for all the wrong reasons
or given credit where there is
none.
I once lived with a woman who
said that I was the funniest man
she had ever met
and she often laughed
when I said something serious.
"oh," she'd laugh, "you ought to be
in the entertainment
business!"
but when I *tried* to be funny
she'd say,
"what the hell do you mean by
that? you're not
funny."

I finally figured it out:
the truth is the funniest thing
around
because you seldom ever hear
it
and when you do
it astonishes you into
laughter.
and when you try to be funny
you often exaggerate the truth
and that's not funny
at all . . .

well, this woman and I
finally separated
and the next one never said whether
I was funny or
not,
she just switched on the

tv
and laughed right along with
the laugh track
while I sat
demeaned and
depressed.

out of the blue

▲▲

she phoned me from a far away
state
"I could never argue with you,"
she told me,
"you'd just run out the door.
my husband's not like that,
he sticks like glue.
he beats me."

"I never believed in discussions,"
I said, "there's nothing to
discuss."

"you're wrong," she said, "you should
try to communicate."

" 'communicate' is an overused word like
'love'," I told her.

"but don't you think two people can
'love'?" she asked.

"not if they try to 'communicate',"
I answered.

"you're talking like an asshole,"
she said.

"we're having an argument,"
I said.

"no," she said, "we're trying to
communicate."

"I've got to leave," I said and hung
up, then took the phone off the
hook.

I looked at the phone.
what they didn't understand was that
sometimes there was nothing to
save
except personal vindication of a
personal viewpoint
and that that was what was going to cause
that blinding white flash
one of these days.

sweater

▲▲

I had to drive to Palos Verdes to do some business at the
savings and loan,
there wasn't much of a line
which was good because there were only two tellers
young ladies
and I got one of them
but she couldn't seem to work
the computer.
sometimes the computer was down.
I waited and watched her struggle.
8 minutes went by.
my lady came back to the window and told me
that the computer wouldn't do something for
her.
"I'm new here," she told
me,
then turning to the other girl
she asked,
"could you help me with this transaction?"
the other girl didn't answer.
my lady tried again: "Louise, would you
please help me with this
transaction?"
"I'll be right back," Louise answered and
closed her window.
she then walked to one of the
tables
where an older woman was talking to a young man
wearing glasses.
Louise stopped about four feet from the
young man
folded her arms and began
listening.
then the young man spoke.
he had on a yellow sweater
only he didn't have it on,
he had it thrown about his shoulders
and the two empty arms hung down over his

267

chest.
they continued to converse as I
watched.
the young man did most of the
talking
and as he did so he swayed
back and forth
ever so slightly
and the arms of his sweater swung
back and forth
back and forth
and he continued to talk and
sway
as I watched the empty arms
of his sweater swing
back and forth.
back and forth.

I don't like people who wear
loose sweaters over their backs
with arms dangling
and these types usually wear
sunglasses pushed back
into their hair
and I could sense
that what he was talking about was
utterly drab
useless
and probably
untrue
and
he had the bland unworried face
of somebody
to whom nothing had happened
yet
and as I watched him sway and
talk
his sweater arms continuing to

swing
Louise stood there
four feet away
arms folded
listening,
and I thought,
this fellow has less
sense
than the common housefly,
and this Louise . . .
likewise.
she knew I was waiting.

I began walking toward
them,
I had to make the first post
at the racetrack
and these three were
being rude, dumb, as if it was a
natural order of business.

I had no idea what I was going to
say
but it was going to be
good.
they stopped talking as I
approached.
then I heard the voice
behind me:
"Mr. Chinaski!"
I stopped,
turned.
"I got the computer to
function!"

I wasn't too happy to
hear that.
I went back to the counter

and we completed the
bookwork.
the girl apologized but
I told her it was
all right.

as I walked toward the
door
I needed to pass the
other three.
they were in the
same positions
and the young man was
still talking
but he no longer
swayed
and the arms of his
yellow sweater
no longer
swung
about.

we'd spoiled each others'
fucking
day.

the skaters

▲▲

I am sitting at a table in the mall drinking coffee while
Linda shops.
I sit above the ice rink where the children skate
in the afternoon,
mostly young girls dressed in blues, reds, whites, greens,
purples, yellows, orange
they are all very good, swift, they spin and glide,
there are no collisions. even the tiniest child
very good, all—
tiny, larger and largest—
whirl through the open spaces as if they were one.

I like it, very much, but then I think
as they get older they will stop skating, they will
stop singing, painting, dancing,
their interests will shift to
survival,
the grace and the gamble will disappear.
but let's not feel too bad:
this happens to animals too:
they play so long
then
stop . . .

then I see Linda, it appears that she has
found something that
pleases her, she rushes toward my table, she
waves,
laughing.
I stand up, wave, smile,
things seem very happy
as down below us they whirl and
glide.
some moments are nice, some are
nicer, some are even worth
writing
about.

about pain

▲▲

my first and only wife
painted
and she talked to me
about it:
"it's all so *painful*
for me, each stroke is
pain . . .
one mistake and
the whole painting is
ruined . . .
you will *never* under-
stand the
pain . . ."

"look, baby," I
said, "why doncha do something easy—
something ya like ta
do?"

she just looked at me
and I think it was her
first understanding of
the tragedy of our being
together.

such things usually
begin
somewhere.

pace is the essence

▲▲

as the mailman walked up the hill
he laughed
when he saw me.
I laughed too.
"yeah, Harry, I know:
just an old man with a hose
watering the parkway.
you got me . . ."

those guys think it's got to be
war
all the time.
I'm just taking a
rest.
when I finally press that red
button
they'll wish I was
back watering the
gladiolas.

green

▲▲

I've been drunk in front of cracked bathroom mirrors
in Southern towns of nowhere
holding a paring knife near the jugular vein and
grinning.
that's when I first learned that stage play is
a great substitute for
reality:
the only separation between doing and
pretending to do
being that infinite hairline of
choice: a
choice between nothing and
nothing.

to awaken in the morning, to
find a place of
employment
where the workers accepted everything
but the dream of
escape.
there were so many places like
that.
there was a job in this town
in Louisiana
which I left each evening
tired and dulled
to that night again
pouring glassfuls and
looking out the
window and
thinking about a girl at
work
in an ill-fitting green dress
who cursed continually about
almost everything.
I only wanted to fuck her
once and
get out of

town.
I only got out of town,
which means I made a choice between
staying nowhere and going
nowhere,
and I imagine if she's alive she's
still cursing about
something
but I no longer hold the paring knife
near the jugular vein—
the end is getting
close enough
all by
itself.

one for the old boy

▲▲

he was just a
cat
cross-eyed,
a dirty white
with pale blue eyes

I won't bore you with his
history
just to say
he had much bad luck
and was a good old
guy
and he died
like people die
like elephants die
like rats die
like flowers die
like water evaporates and
the wind stops blowing

the lungs gave out
last Monday.
now he's in the rose
garden
and I've heard a
stirring march
playing for him
inside of me
which I know
not many
but some of you
would like to
know
about.

that's
all.

eating my senior citizen's dinner at the Sizzler

▲▲

between 2 and 5 p.m. any day and any time on Sunday and
Wednesday, it's 20% off for
us old dogs approaching the sunset.
it's strange to be old and not feel
old
but I glance in the mirror
see some silver hair
concede that I'd look misplaced at a
rock concert.

I eat alone.
the other oldies are in groups,
a man and a woman
a woman and a woman
three old women
another man and a
woman.
it's 4:30 p.m. on a
Tuesday
and just 5 or 6 blocks north is
the cemetery
on a long sloping green hill,
a very modern place with
the markers
flat on the ground,
it's much more pleasant for
passing traffic.

a young waitress
moves among us
filling our cups
again with lovely
poisonous caffeine.
we thank her and
chew on,
some with our own
teeth.

we wouldn't lose much in a
nuclear explosion.

one good old boy talks
on and on
about what
he's not too
sure.

well, I finish my meal,
leave a tip.
I have the last table by the
exit door.
as I'm about to leave
I'm blocked by an old girl
in a walker
followed by another old girl
whose back is bent
like a bow.
their faces, their arms
their hands are like
parchment
as if they had already been
embalmed
but they leave quietly.

as I made ready to leave
again
I am blocked
this time by a huge
wheelchair
the back tilted low
it's almost like a bed,
a very expensive
mechanism,
an awesome and glorious
receptacle
the chrome glitters

and the thick tires are
air-inflated
and the lady in the chair and
the lady pushing it
look alike,
sisters no doubt,
one's lucky
gets to ride,
and they go by
again very *white*.

and then
I rise
make it to the door
into stunning sunlight
make it to the car
get in
roar the engine into
life
rip it into reverse
with a quick back turn of squealing
tires
I slam to a bouncing halt
rip the wheel right
feed the gas
go from first to second
spin into a gap of
traffic
am quickly into
3rd
4th
I am up to
50 mph in a flash
moving through
them.
who can turn the stream
of destiny?
I light a cigarette

punch on the radio
and a young girl
sings,
"put it where it hurts,
daddy, make me love
you . . ."

Photo, Richard Robinson.

Photo: Richard Robinson

CHARLES BUKOWSKI is one of America's best-known contemporary writers of poetry and prose, and, many would claim, its most influential and imitated poet. He was born in Andernach, Germany, to an American soldier father and a German mother in 1920, and brought to the United States at the age of three. He was raised in Los Angeles and lived there for fifty years. He published his first story in 1944 when he was twenty-four and began writing poetry at the age of thirty-five. He died in San Pedro, California, on March 9, 1994, at the age of seventy-three, shortly after completing his last novel, *Pulp* (1994).

During his lifetime he published more than forty-five books of poetry and prose, including the novels *Post Office* (1971), *Factotum* (1975), *Women* (1978), *Ham on Rye* (1982), and *Hollywood* (1989). Among his most recent books are the posthumous editions of *What Matters Most Is How Well You Walk Through the Fire* (1999), *Open All Night: New Poems* (2000), *Beerspit Night and Cursing: The Correspondence of Charles Bukowski and Sheri Martinelli, 1960–1967* (2001), and *Night Torn Mad with Footsteps: New Poems* (2001).

All of his books have now been published in translation in more than a dozen languages and his worldwide popularity remains undiminished. In the years to come Ecco will publish additional volumes of previously uncollected poetry and letters.

THESE AND OTHER TITLES BY CHARLES BUKOWSKI
ARE AVAILABLE FROM

ecco *An Imprint of* HarperCollins*Publishers*

ISBN 0-06-057705-3 (hc)
ISBN 0-06-057706-1 (pb)

ISBN 0-06-057703-7 (hc)
ISBN 0-06-057704-5 (pb)

ISBN 0-06-057701-0 (hc)
ISBN 0-06-057702-9 (pb)

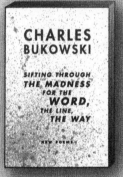

ISBN 0-06-052735-8 (hc)
ISBN 0-06-056823-2 (pb)

ISBN 0-876-85557-5 (pb)

ISBN 0-876-85362-9 (pb)

ISBN 0-876-85086-7 (pb)

ISBN 0-876-85926-0 (pb)

ISBN 0-876-85390-4 (pb)

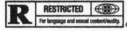